WHEN THE GREAT
RED DAWN IS SHINING

CHRISTOPHER J. A. MORRY

WHEN THE GREAT RED DAWN IS SHINING

Howard L. Morry's Memoirs of Life in the
Newfoundland Regiment

Compiled and edited by

CHRISTOPHER J. A. MORRY

Breakwater Books
PO Box 2188, St. John's, NL, Canada A1C 6E6
www.breakwaterbooks.com

Library and Archives Canada Cataloguing in Publication
Morry, Christopher, 1949-, author

When the great red dawn is shining : Howard Morry's memoirs of life
in the Newfoundland Regiment / Christopher Morry.
ISBN 978-1-55081-563-4 (bound)

1. Morry, Howard, 1885-1972. 2. Beaumont-Hamel, Battle of, Beaumont-Hamel,
France, 1916—Personal narratives, Canadian. 3. Beaumont-Hamel, Battle of,
Beaumont-Hamel, France, 1916—Personal narratives, British. 4. Somme, 1st
Battle of the, France, 1916—Personal narratives, Canadian. 5. Somme, 1st Battle
of the, France, 1916—Personal narratives, British. 6. Soldiers—Newfoundland
and Labrador—Biography. 7. Great Britain. Army. Newfoundland Regiment,
1st—Biography. I. Morry, Howard, 1885-1972, author II. Title.
D640.M647M67 2014   940.4'81718   C2014-901926-2

Cover design: Rhonda Molloy
Interior design: John van der Woude Designs

Previous page: *Shadow box of war memorabilia belonging to Howard Leopold Morry,
now in the possession of his grandson, Howard Glendon Morry.*

We acknowledge the support of the Canada Council for the Arts, which last year invested
$154 million to bring the arts to Canadians throughout the country. We acknowledge
the Government of Canada through the Canada Book Fund and the Government
of Newfoundland and Labrador through the Department of Tourism, Culture and
Recreation for our publishing activities.

Canada

Canada Council   Conseil des Arts
for the Arts   du Canada

Newfoundland
Labrador

Printed and Bound in Canada.

To those brave Newfoundland men of the RNR *who fought for King and Country in* WWI—*for those who died, and for those who came home wounded, more often in mind and soul than in body.*

WHEN THE GREAT RED DAWN IS SHINING (3).

Dark is the world, but still I wait and pray
Through ev'ry hour to see the rising day—
That golden day that dawns on grief and pain,
That day of love that calls me home again.

When the great red dawn is shining,
When the waiting hours are past,
When the tears of night are ended
And I see the day at last,
I shall come down the road of sunshine,
To a heart that is fond and true,
When the great red dawn is shining,
Back to home, back to love, and you.

"When the Great Red Dawn Is Shining"
Lyrics by Edward Lockton and music by Evelyn Sharpe

Contents

Acknowledgements

A book such as this, built upon the written recollections of one man, depended upon the labours of many people to make its publication a reality. Howard Leopold Morry (Dad Morry) was a prodigious diarist. We, his children and grandchildren, are fortunate to have discovered and preserved many, though not all, of his diaries. Some were lost or destroyed many years ago, but what we do have fills twenty-two notebooks and a number of lengthy letters to his children. Over the years, a number of us have dedicated our time to transcribe these diaries so they can be better preserved and shared. The work is still not complete. Those who have participated in this task up until now include my late cousin, Jamie Morry, my cousin Karen Chapman (née Funkhouser), and my brother Glen and I. We also owe a debt of gratitude to an unfortunately anonymous librarian at the Provincial Library (now the A. C. Hunter Library) in St. John's who was the first to begin the task of transcribing and recording, on a manual typewriter, one of the most crucial war diaries sometime in the early 1960s. Our late aunt Elsie Ranger (née Morry) and my cousin Howie Morry, Jamie's brother, have also been the careful custodians of a number of these diaries, and my cousin, Fredi Caines (née Mercer), is the custodian and protector of a large collection of Dad Morry's photos and memorabilia. Our late aunt, Jean Funkhouser (née Morry), Karen's mother, not only preserved a number of the diaries, but was also inspired by Dad Morry to become the first in the family to make a dedicated effort to research and record the family history, including the larger-than-life role he played in it.

Staff at the Centre for Newfoundland Studies, Memorial University of Newfoundland, the Provincial Archives of Newfoundland and Labrador (now a division of The Rooms), and Library and Archives Canada all provided invaluable assistance in completing the background research needed to compile the historical facts mentioned in my explanatory notes.

Three authors of books previously published on the topic of the Royal Newfoundland Regiment in World War One—Gary Browne, Bert Riggs, and Frank Gogos—discussed the concept of this book with me and offered constructive ideas and great encouragement to pursue the goal of seeing Dad Morry's memoirs published. Graham Skanes, Chair of the Museum Committee of the RNR Museum in St. John's, also assisted with conflicts between Dad Morry's account and the historical record.

Larry Coady, a very good friend and frequent hiking companion and also, happily, a past president of the Newfoundland Historical Society, kindly accepted the task of providing preliminary editorial comments.

The many volunteers who have contributed countless hours of their time to assemble military and historical information freely available on the *Newfoundland's Grand Banks* website deserve many thanks for facilitating this research.

For a first time author, the constant assistance, thoroughly professional advice and kind consideration offered by Rebecca Rose, president and publisher, James Langer, managing editor, and Rhonda Molloy, graphic design specialist, at Breakwater Books has made this journey not only much easier but also a truly enjoyable experience.

It is a universal truth that the preparation of a book, even one already drafted in large measure by another person, requires a great deal of time—time stolen from one's own family. Therefore I owe a special thanks to my wife, Jamie, and our children—Nicola, Prema, and Bryan—who consistently encouraged me in this endeavour.

Preface

The awesome and terrible events of WWI that ultimately led to Newfoundland's first Regiment having bestowed upon it the title of "Royal" by King George V have been told and retold countless times. For the average Newfoundlander, even for young people three generations removed from the actual events, these images are vivid, though obviously not as indelibly imprinted in their minds as they were in the minds of those who fought and suffered on the fields of battle in Gallipoli, France, and Belgium.

Before reviewing the literature already available on this topic, it would perhaps be useful for those less familiar with the Royal Newfoundland Regiment to provide an extremely brief account of its history. This subject has been covered in far greater detail in several of the books mentioned below, and the reader is referred to them for greater detail.

Nowadays, when many people think about the Royal Newfoundland Regiment (RNR), they immediately think of World War I. In reality, the regiment has existed in one form or another, with various periods of stand down, since it was initially formed under Colonel Thomas Skinner of the Royal Engineers in 1795. At that time, it had not earned the title "Royal," but it is a little known fact that it did earn the honour more than once: as alluded to above, during WWI, but also previously as recognition of the important role the regiment played in defeating the American forces in a number of pivotal battles in the War of 1812. It was also almost certainly an unknown fact to Howard Morry when he joined the regiment in 1914 that he was a distant relative of Colonel Skinner's. Colonel Skinner's great-granddaughter, Elizabeth Sarah Winsor, was Howard's grandaunt by marriage.

During much of the 1800s, the regiment was retired, and it was the lack of such a military body at the outbreak of WWI that made it so difficult for Newfoundland to mount the forces it had promised to help in the defence of Britain. Not that it was difficult to raise recruits; far from it. The initial call to arms resulted in the "First 500," the volunteers needed to meet the initial promise to Britain, coming forward in less than two weeks. But these were far from seasoned veterans, being, at best, members of one of the largely church-led brigades of militia that existed at the time, such as the Anglican Church Lads' Brigade, the Methodist Guards, the Catholic Cadet Corps, the Newfoundland Highlanders, and the Legion of Frontiersmen—irregulars without a common uniform and with very little military training in most cases. Indeed, it was because of their irregular uniforms that the First 500 wound up being referred to as the "Blue Puttees," a reference to their non-standard-issue leggings, borrowed from the Church Lads' Brigade.

While these informal paramilitary groups initially formed the backbone of the regiment to be sent overseas, their ranks were augmented by the sons of wealthy merchants and ordinary shopkeepers from St. John's and hardy weathered fishermen and foresters from around the bay to form a fighting force of 1000. An unusual mix, but one that soon united with pride and the confidence that they could overcome whatever challenges were thrown their way.

There was little time to waste, and training in Newfoundland prior to departure was elementary to say the least. Their first taste of real training came in Scotland, where they were sent to garrison Edinburgh Castle, a singular honour, and then later at Stobs Camp nearby. Training continued in southern England at Aldershot and on Salisbury Plains just prior to embarking, and they were seasoned for hot weather combat in Egypt before finally being sent to the Peninsula to fight alongside of the ANZACs (Australia-New Zealand Army Corps) and other colonial and British forces and their allies. Their aim—to wrest control of a vital water body, the Dardanelles, away from the Turks so as to allow the British allies, namely Russia, to send their warships from the Crimea on the Black Sea into the Mediterranean and Atlantic to engage German warships and U-boats. As history tells us, the effort was a colossal failure, costing many lives, not only in battle, but through disease that ran rampant in the trenches, and exposure to harsh environmental conditions. Newfoundland suffered its first casualties in the war in that theatre (thirty soldiers of the regiment were killed or mortally wounded in action, and ten died of disease) before finally playing a pivotal role as the rearguard at both the Suvla Bay and Cape Helles evacuations.

The regiment went on to fight in many other theatres of war in France and Belgium and earned battle honours at Gallipoli, Beaumont-Hamel (Albert), Le Transloy, Arras, Ypres (1917 and 1918), Langemarck, Poelcapelle, Cambrai, Bailleul, Courtrai, all of which are emblazoned on their colours, and other locations including Guedecourt, Monchy-le-Preux, Stenebeek, Broombeek, Masnieres, Marcoing, and Ledeghem. As everyone knows, the greatest loss of life for the Newfoundlanders, and for the British forces that fought alongside of them, took place at the infamous Battle of Beaumont-Hamel, a poorly planned and even more poorly executed attempt to break through the stalemate in the opposed allied and German front lines on the Somme River. As is often quoted, the regiment went in with twenty-two officers and 758 other ranks, but only sixty-eight were able to answer the roll call afterwards, the rest either dead or seriously wounded.

Strangely, in Newfoundland it remains this sad defeat that is most remembered and commemorated every July 1, the anniversary of the battle. But the Newfoundland Regiment went on to earn its "Royal" title in costly but courageous and glorious victories at Cambrai and Ypres in particular.

After peace was declared, the Regiment was not disbanded but maintained as a home-based militia. Because of this, it was much easier to muster a contingent when the call to arms came at the outset of World War II. However, in that war Newfoundland was not afforded the opportunity to field its own regiment, and the troops sent over to fight formed a part of other British regiments, notably in the artillery.

Since WWII, and especially since Confederation in 1949, the regiment has continued once again as a smaller militia and has contributed volunteers for peacekeeping and armed forces required to meet the challenges faced by the Canadian Army overseas.

There have been more than a score of books published recounting the history of the Royal Newfoundland Regiment (RNR) in WWI. As we commemorate the centenary of the outbreak of that war this year, several more books covering the subject will undoubtedly appear.

During the war, readers at home in Newfoundland were updated, to the extent that the censors allowed, by articles written for *The Daily News* from the trenches by Francis T. (Mayo) Lind. "Mayo" received his moniker when his pleas for Mayo cigarette tobacco for the men in the trenches met with an overwhelming show of support from the home front. He was thirty-five when he enlisted, had a natural flair for writing, and thus wound up becoming a *de facto* war correspondent. It was the practice of the day for government censors to only reveal good news to the home front, and even then only many days or weeks after the events had taken place. Mayo filled in some of the gaps, though he was careful to self-censor his reports so as to not unduly alarm loved ones at home. Regrettably, Mayo and hundreds of his comrades in arms were killed on the field of battle on July 1, 1916, at Beaumont-Hamel. In 2001, in cooperation with the Royal Newfoundland Regiment, Creative Publishers (Killick Press) in St. John's compiled Mayo's articles from *The Daily News* and published an anthology in commemoration of the eighty-fifth anniversary of that infamous battle under the title *The Letters of Mayo Lind.*

The first actual book published on the RNR in World War I, *Trenching at Gallipoli: The Personal Narrative of a Newfoundlander with the Ill-fated Dardanelles Expedition*, by John Gallishaw, a foot soldier invalided out after Gallipoli, appeared in 1916, just before Beaumont-Hamel, the tragic battle that forever defines the bravery and patriotism of the common Newfoundland soldier. Gallishaw, unlike most in the trenches, was college educated in the US and therefore wrote with a polished style that would not be possible for the average foot soldier. On the other hand, that more polished writing style brought with it a certain reticence to be blunt and frank about the conditions the men faced, which took some of the emotion out of the retelling of events.

Since that time, books have appeared at regular intervals in an attempt to find meaning in the savagery and hardships endured by the ordinary enlisted men of the RNR. One of the most comprehensive accounts, as well as one of the earliest, was the work of Richard Cramm, *The First Five Hundred: Being a Historical Sketch of the Military Operations of the Royal Newfoundland Regiment in Gallipoli and on the Western Front*, which appeared in 1921 after the hostilities had ended. Cramm took great pains to outline events, but also to provide as much supporting personal information as possible, including in some cases photographs of the members of the First 500, who carried with pride the title of "The Blue Puttees." That moniker was originally bestowed on them by the British Tommys as a term of derision regarding their hastily prepared kit. The regulation issue uniforms were not readily available as so many volunteers rushed to answer the call to arms. The RNR's kit included blue rather than khaki puttees, and so the epithet stuck, but became a badge of honour for those who proudly bore it.

In 1933, R. H. Tait, MC, published a lengthy poem about the RNR in WWI—*The Trail of The Caribou: The Royal Newfoundland Regiment, 1914-1918*. Although printed twice that year and published again the following year by the same company, this book is long out of print and now difficult to find. Then Major R. H. (Bert) Tait had been the lieutenant who led the regimental colours onto the ss *Florizel* on October 3, 1914, when the first troops embarked to sail from Newfoundland to Europe. In Tait's book, the poem itself is contextualized at the end by comments from the author. Here is an excerpt that commemorates the deeds of Newfoundland's most famous soldier, the Royal Newfoundland Regiment's only Victoria Cross recipient, Tommy Ricketts:

> *Here Ricketts won immortal fame*
> *And added lustre to the name*
> *Of Newfoundland. This but a lad,*
> *Who scarcely sixteen summers had,*
> *Mere youth in years, but man at heart,*
> *Was called to play a hero's part.*
> *Did hero prove? The King's V.C.,*
> *The highest crown for gallantry,*
> *Was his award, and our proud boast—*
> *This fisher lad from northern coast.*

The book/poem covered the entire period of wwi from 1914 to 1918. In a sense, this was the first of two accounts of the battles recorded from the perspective of an officer who experienced these events (see Facey-Crowther's book, based on Lieutenant Owen Steele's letters home, mentioned below) and therefore portrayed a different perspective than that of the men in the trenches.

These early accounts have been supplemented over the years by other authors whose perspectives differed and who therefore added different dimensions to the tale. In 1964, Col. Gerald W.L. Nicholson, who had served with the Prince Albert Volunteers and had been a historian in the Canadian Army, provided what might best be described as an "official" view of the battles fought by the rnr—*The Fighting Newfoundlander: A History of the Royal Newfoundland Regiment*. This work was commissioned by the Newfoundland Government to commemorate the fiftieth anniversary of the First 500 leaving St. John's. One unique element of the book is the coverage of the regiment's entire history from the War of 1812 right through to WWII. As an officer himself, Nicholson naturally saw things from the perspective of those in charge. While this is a useful perspective for many reasons, it must be remembered that the common soldier did not see things in quite the same light. One stark example is found in his praise of the leadership of Lt. Col. Arthur Lovell Hadow CMG, who led the RNR into battle at Beaumont-Hamel. In fact, contrary to the suggestions by Nicholson and others who have reported from the officers' perspective, Howard Morry's memoirs clearly reveal that Hadow was universally despised by the men and was thought to have directly contributed in large measure to the miseries they endured, and perhaps even to the toll in terms of casualties and loss of life. Nicholson made his interpretation based on what I believe was a misunderstanding of the words of a number of wounded soldiers as they were being taken from the battlefield after the battle of Beaumont-Hamel. Capt. Raley, Hadow's adjutant, is reported by Nicholson to have heard the men say, " Is the Colonel satisfied?" and took this to mean that the men were seriously hoping that their doomed efforts were up to the impossibly high standards of their Colonel. An alternative, and possibly more plausible explanation, does not seem to have occurred to either Raley or Nicholson. The men may very well have been cynically suggesting that this disaster was entirely the fault of Col. Hadow. The fact that Hadow was an advisor to Nicholson in the preparation of this book would tend to ensure this latter interpretation would not be considered. Other authors since, including Joy B. Cave, have repeated Nicholson's interpretation without questioning the alternate possibility. Years later, after the war was over, it is reported by Howard Morry that Col. Hadow came to a reunion in Newfoundland expecting to be welcomed with open arms by the RNR veterans. Instead, he was shunned and is said to have left in tears.

On the other hand, if this is seen as a flaw in Col. Nicholson's reporting, it is more than counterbalanced by the fact that he lends the authority of an accomplished military historian, which is not the case for many of the other published accounts. The book was republished by McGill-Queen's University Press in 2006 with a new introduction by Prof. David R. Facey-Crowther, a testament to the document's historical value.

More than a decade later, Joy Cave provided a different twist to the story. Cave narrowed the focus to examine the RNR's war record, especially the tragic yet glorious events surrounding the "July Drive," in her book *What Became of Corporal Pittman?* Though she dedicated great energy to researching the events themselves, her imagination supplied the details of what those final hours and minutes might have been like for those who went over the top. Her account was very personal; she visited the battle sites with her seventeen-year-old daughter and tried desperately to explain these events to her. They searched for the gravesites and memorials erected for the fallen of the RNR, and particularly focussed their efforts on one whose grave was difficult to find due to a misspelling of his name in the official records—"Corporal Richard Pitman." Cave could not rely on the testimony of Richard Pittman to write her story because he was one of the many who lost their lives and whose bodies were never found after the Battle of Beaumont-Hamel, and he had not written any memoirs before his death. Despite these limitations, Cave's accounts come much closer to the reality of what warfare in those times meant for common soldiers from outport Newfoundland. The book was written in large measure as an attempt to explain the unexplainable to her daughter and the youth of her day. How could an ordinary young man of much the same upbringing as themselves be expected to take on the role of hero in such overwhelmingly impossible circumstances? Her unnamed daughter could not find a fully satisfactory answer, and no doubt each young reader would take away different thoughts on the subject. There are no easy answers.

There was an apparent lull in interest in the exploits of the RNR for a couple of decades after this, as evidenced by an absence of new publications on the topic. As a non-specialist in the field of sociology, I am tempted to associate this with the times—the mid-1970s to mid-1980s—when the baby boomer generation (the "me" generation) was in its heyday and "live for today" was the byword. It does seem that during this period of time Canadians in general, and not just Newfoundlanders, apparently wanted to put the past behind them. Turn-outs at the National War Memorial on November 11 and at the Provincial War Memorial on July 1 declined during that time and only began to pick up again in more recent years. Whatever the reasons, that lull passed and since then interest is stronger than ever.

In 1991, two books appeared that, to some extent, reignited interest in the RNR. David Macfarlane wrote a family history of the Goodyears entitled *The Danger Tree*. The title was of course an allusion to that infamous tree which, in skeletal form stripped of its branches and leaves by shell fire, marked the RNR's farthest point of advance into No Man's Land at Beaumont-Hamel. The Goodyears, like many other families from Newfoundland, gained the dubious distinction of losing multiple members of their family on the battlefields of Europe in WWI. Though providing useful details on the stories of these soldiers, this book provides only a passing glimpse at the effects of the war on this family, while recounting other historical events that also impacted them over the years before and after the war.

In the same year, Tony Murphy and Paul Kenney co-authored a pictorial account entitled *The Trail of the Caribou: Newfoundland in the First World War 1914-1918* (not to be confused with Tait's earlier work mentioned above), utilising many previously archived and unavailable photographs taken during the war.

In 1994, the book considered by most authorities to be one of the most comprehensive and exhaustive analyses of the history of the RNR hit the bookshelves. In that year, W. David Parsons published a modestly captioned "guide" to the RNR in WWI—*Pilgrimage: A Guide to the Royal Newfoundland Regiment in World War One*. Dr. Parsons (MD, CM, FRCP) provides a clinical analysis worthy of the physician of note that he is. His work parallels in many ways the earlier treatise by Col. Nicholson, but is not encumbered with the optics of an officer interpreting the actions of other officers and provides a balanced point of view. Because it is more academic in approach, some may find it lacks the emotional impact that other first-hand accounts possess.

The following year, in 1995, David R. Facey-Crowther trumped the work of Parsons, at least in terms of the time scale, by assembling, as editor, documentation which details the entire 200 year history of the RNR from its earliest days to the present time. This work, entitled *Better than the Best: The Story of the Royal Newfoundland Regiment, 1795-1995,* was carried out in cooperation with the Royal Newfoundland Regiment Advisory Council to commemorate the 200th anniversary of the Regiment.

If the 1990's represented a reawakening of interest in the RNR, the millennium represented a total rebirth. Since 2000, in addition to the republication of many of the more important works mentioned above, ten entirely new treatments have been added to the bibliography of the RNR.

The first of these was *The Memoirs of a Blue Puttee: The Newfoundland Regiment in WWI.* This was a first-hand account of an enlisted man, James Anthony Stacey, as retold by his daughter in law, Jean Edwards Stacey, and was based largely upon his own memoirs. As one soldier on the ground could not possibly have an overall picture of how the war was playing out, Jean Stacey supplemented her father-in-law's memoirs thoroughly with well-researched details of the war overall. The author's addition of this explanatory material in no way diminished this book in its essentials as an informed perspective from one who lived through it.

Following in 2003, David Facey-Crowther revisited the war, this time from the perspective of Lieutenant Owen William Steele in *Lieutenant Owen William Steele of the Newfoundland Regiment: Diary and Letters.* Owen Steele was one of the First 500, enlisting at the outbreak of hostilities as a private, rising through the ranks quickly, and finally being commissioned in the field as a lieutenant. He recorded his observations, as much as the censors would allow, in letters home and in personal diaries. These were edited and assembled with an added family history provided by Owen's nephew, James. Owen Steele's story ended when he died from wounds inflicted by an exploding German shell on July 7, 1916, just six days after he survived the battle of Beaumont-Hamel. Although his story covers only about half of the years that the RNR fought in WWI, this account adds a new dimension to the earlier histories because it shows the changing viewpoint of a man taking on increasing responsibility as the events of war enveloped him.

Norm Christie had been publishing his *For King and Empire* series of books on Canadian soldiers in WWI for more than a decade and had already published nine such books when, in 2003, he came out with his tenth, entitled *The Newfoundlanders in the Great War: The Western Front, 1916-1918*. Christie wrote as a historian, but one with a rather unique perspective. He had acted as the records officer for the Commonwealth War Graves Commission in London and was therefore familiar with the actual battle sites and places of burial of Commonwealth soldiers. Each of his earlier books focussed on a single battle in which Canadian soldiers fought, and these books provided details on memorials and cemeteries for the benefit of those wishing to visit these locations. He followed much the same pattern in his tenth account, which focussed on the RNR, with the exception that he provided details on all of their engagements in the Western theatre of war (excluding Gallipoli).

Also in 2003, Francis Patey, who was born on the Northern Peninsula and had previously written five books concerning various aspects of life in that particular part of Newfoundland, focused on the role of Northern Peninsula and Labrador men at war in his book *Veterans of the North*. The book is unique in that it deals with Northern Peninsula and Labrador men fighting in all major theatres of war of the twentieth century in which Newfoundlanders and Canadians were involved. This included chapters on WWI, WWII, Korea, and the Gulf War. By dealing with these four conflicts in one analysis, Patey provides a completely different and wider focus on the gallantry and the sacrifices of Newfoundland men at war over the years.

Almost all of the above accounts at one point or another make mention of the important role that Padre Thomas Nangle played during WWI, comforting soldiers heading into battle and most especially caring for the spiritual needs of the wounded and the dying. Few mentioned, however, his contribution, during and after the war, in ensuring the preservation of the last resting place of the fallen Newfoundlanders, and in seeing to it that the locations of their major sacrifices were remembered with suitable memorials. Gary Browne and Darren McGrath set about correcting this oversight in 2006 with the publication of Padre Nangle's life story: *Soldier Priest in the Killing Fields of Europe: Padre Thomas Nangle, Chaplain to the Newfoundland Regiment in WWI.* It was Nangle who undertook the horrific task of recovering the corpses of Newfoundland soldiers left on the battlefields without proper Christian burial, sometimes for months or years. It was also he who fought tirelessly to raise the funds and overcome the hurdles of acquiring the most sacred ground for the five major memorials erected to commemorate the deeds and the losses of the RNR in France and Belgium. He was also instrumental in planning and in raising the needed funds to engage British sculptor, Capt. Basil Gotto, to create the magnificent bronze statue of a trumpeting male caribou (the "Monarch of the Topsails") that serves as the centre point of each memorial. This view of war is unique, and without it the story of the RNR in WWI would be incomplete.

In an effort similar in many ways to the publishing of the letters of Mayo Lind, Bert Riggs edited and published, in 2007, fifty-one letters written by Corporal Curtis Forsey in the book *Grand Bank Soldier: The War Letters of Lance Corporal Curtis Forsey.* The difference in this case is that Cpl. Forsey joined up late in the war, and his accounts therefore focus on the period after Beaumont-Hamel, a topic not well covered by earlier accounts.

In 2009, Frank Gogos and Morgan MacDonald set about to correct another oversight in their book, *Known unto God: In Honour of Newfoundland's Missing During the Great War,* as they focused on all of the fallen Newfoundlanders: not just those in the RNR, but also the sailors who joined the Royal Navy and Merchant Marine and gave their lives in engagements at sea. When one considers how closely the history of Newfoundland is attached to seafaring, it is a wonder how these contributions had all but been forgotten prior to the publishing of this book. The material is essentially pictorial with brief written annotations, and there is room for a more in-depth account of this aspect of Newfoundland at war. The authors quoted from Howard Leopold Morry's diaries to describe the horror of the aftermath of the Battle of Beaumont-Hamel.

In 2010, two new books appeared on bookshelves that dealt with unique or specific aspects of the Newfoundland contributions and losses in WWI. Gary Browne took up pen once again to examine the saddest of all losses during those years by retelling the stories of the young and often underage boy soldiers who gave their lives for their country in *Forget-Me-Not: Fallen Boy Soldiers*. Browne has enriched his telling of their stories with firsthand accounts written by many of their fellow soldiers who stood beside them at the moment of their deaths, including Howard Leopold Morry.

Anthony McAllister concentrated on a single battle, Monchy-le-Preux, in *The Greatest Gallantry: The Newfoundland Regiment at Monchy-le-Preux April 14, 1917*. Newfoundlanders are not as familiar with the uplifting story of the heroes of Monchy as they are with the tragedy that unfolded at Beaumont-Hamel. While the losses incurred by the RNR at Monchy were by no means comparable to the disaster at Beaumont-Hamel, the gallantry and bravery demonstrated at Monchy was impressive and worthy of note. It was at the battle of Monchy that nine Newfoundlanders and one British Tommy stood their ground and held this vital town from being retaken by a far superior force of Germans.

In 2011, Jack Fitzgerald, a well-known herald of things Newfoundland, who has written over a dozen books on various subjects pertaining to the province, turned his attention to the subject of Newfoundland during WWI. Specifically, he focussed on an aspect of the war on the home front that had not been well recounted in early treatments, the threat to Newfoundland and to allied shipping posed by German U-boats, in his work *The Spring Rice Document: Newfoundland at War 1914-1918*. He noted that, prior to going overseas, some elements of the RNR were dispatched to the Northern Peninsula in an attempt to prevent the Germans from establishing a submarine base there or in Labrador. While German submarines inflicted serious harm on allied shipping, both military and merchant vessels in North American waters, no supply stations were ever established. Fitzgerald turned his attention in the rest of the book to his own account of the RNR overseas with an emphasis on key battles such as Beaumont-Hamel and Cambrai, as well as a brief account of how returning soldiers were treated after the war.

In 2012, Joan Sullivan, editor of the *Newfoundland Quarterly*, published another personal account of the war, this time from the perspective of Lieutenant Stephen Norris of Three Arms Island, NDB, simply titled *In the Field*. Lieut. Norris's story is compelling for a number of reasons. First, he was an officer well respected by his men, which was not always the case in those days. His loss to a German shell the day before the fateful battle of Guedecourt was sorely felt by his fellow Newfoundland soldiers. It was also a disaster for his tiny home town. His family ran the community's only business, which not only supplied all their daily needs, but bought their fish for market. When Stephen died, his father lost interest in the business that was to be inherited by Stephen after the war. With the closing of the business, the community eventually withered away. Sullivan tells his story, but also updates it with information on a play written and performed by students and staff at Gonzaga High School in St. John's and tells the story of how the performance brought the disparate elements of the Norris family back together again after many years.

Other books, including novels (e.g., Kevin Major's *No Man's Land* and Earl Pilgrim's *Freddy Frieda Goes to War*), have been written on the subject of the RNR in WWI, but those briefly summarized above represent the most important accounts, covering as they do many perspectives and focusing on many specific or unique details that might otherwise have been forgotten. Several of the above incorporate brief passages from the diaries of Howard Leopold Morry (e.g., *Forget-Me-Not: Fallen Boy Soldiers* and *Known Unto God*) to illustrate a point or a perspective perhaps not dealt with completely in the main thrust of their narrative. One might ask, therefore, if there is room for another view of these dramatic and proud, but sad, elements of Newfoundland's history. Is there anything missing from the telling of this tale that could possibly be corrected by one more examination of these events? I believe there is.

Howard Leopold Morry was not a boy soldier—far from it! When he enlisted on December 17, 1914, he was already twenty-nine years old—an old man by the standards of the common enlisted soldier. Furthermore, though he listed his profession on his attestation papers as "fisherman," that was a great over-simplification of his position in the small society of Ferryland from whence he hailed. In point of fact, he was the scion of a merchant-class family that had occupied a position of importance on the southern shore for four generations before him, but whose fortune was wiped out in the great Newfoundland bank collapse of 1894, when he was just a boy. In addition, he was not inexperienced in things pertaining to the rest of the world, as were most of his fellow soldiers, having beaten around western Canada with his brothers for some years before the call to arms brought each of them to different recruiting stations, either in Canada or Newfoundland.

But most importantly, Dad Morry, as he will forever be known by the family, had a natural gift for storytelling. Whether this was a refinement of the oral history telling common to outports across Newfoundland or an undeveloped and unutilized talent as a potential author, he could not help but record everything he saw around him in words or in writing. And later in life, when the time became available, he drew upon this wonderful skill to leave to future generations dozens of notebooks in which he recorded his observations on the history of the Southern Shore, everyday life in olden times, his adventures in the wheat fields of the prairies and the salmon canneries and fishing boats of BC, and all manner of other observations. Hidden amongst these many notebooks he also recorded in graphic and at times disturbing, but also sometimes amusing detail his experiences while overseas in WWI. These anecdotes appeared spread over many of his notebooks, which took the form of daily diaries in which, from time to time, when work was slow during the winter months in particular, he would take the opportunity to jot down some memory or another.

The first effort to put down his memories of the war years ranged across four of his notebooks dating from December 1939, when he was fifty-four, until January 1950. Later again, starting in 1957, when he was in his seventies, he took the time to draw many of these fragmentary reminiscences together into not one, but two comprehensive accounts of his war experiences. In one of those two versions, Dad Morry penned a note to my father, Thomas Graham Morry: "Take care of this book—'twill be interesting for your grandchildren to read by and by. 'Twas a great experience, boy. Not many of the Dardanelles bunch left right now." How those words now seem prophetic.

And again—in a lengthy and detailed letter to his daughter, Jean, in 1961—he recorded his memories of these events as well as much more of his life story. The present text draws from all of these sources, as well as our family's memories of Dad Morry's retelling of these events on his visits to his children and grandchildren dispersed over North America. I believe readers familiar with earlier accounts will find his story makes an important contribution at the emotional level to our understanding of what it was like to be an ordinary foot soldier in the RNR on the battlefields and in the trenches of Gallipoli and the Western Front. His comments on the government's post-war treatment of Newfoundland veterans also add a poignant footnote to the histories already written by others.

One final editorial comment is required here. My grandfather was a product of the time and place that produced him, and there were aspects of his attitude toward other races that are no longer common nor acceptable in our society. Call it prejudice or bigotry, he was no different in this respect than many others with a similar upbringing in outport Newfoundland in those times. But because some of his words would be offensive in the context of today's more enlightened public attitudes, I have been persuaded that it would be best to remove the more offensive words and phrases. I struggled with the decision whether or not such censorship was acceptable in presenting this historical narrative, but in the end I do believe that not doing so would dishonour my grandfather's memory. He himself would not have held or spoken these views had he been raised half a century later.

Howard Leopold Morry and his diaries. Photo collage by Christopher Morry.

1

Beginnings

To fully understand the kind of man that Howard Leopold Morry was, and therefore to be able to place in proper context his reporting on the events he lived through with the RNR in WWI, one must first know a little about his background and upbringing. Luckily, he took the time on several occasions in his life to record his remembrances of his early years, as well as his time overseas. He begins one such memoir with the following:

Ferryland Dec 12, 1939

Having long been thinking of writing an outline of the principle events of the time and the everyday life of the people of this little place, and the events that have happened to my remembrance, and some of the happenings of my own life. Now being in my 55th year and having an 80 percent heart disability through services in the Great War of 1914 to 1918, if I put off writing any longer it will be too late, for my expectations of a long life are pretty limited. So on this 12th day of December, 1939, being a wet day with a gale of a N Northeaster and with some time on my hands and hoping it will be of some interest to those who come after me, when I have said my little piece and passed behind the veil, I will begin.

Howard Leopold Morry was born in Ferryland on July 24, 1885, the son of Thomas Graham Morry and Catherine Frances White. The Morry family first came to Newfoundland on a seasonal basis sometime in the mid to late 1700s as part of the well-developed West Country fishery out of Dartmouth, Devon. Initially, they served as mates and skippers on the fishing vessels owned by the famous merchants of that town: the Newmans, Holdsworths, Searles, and others. But by 1774 they had managed to accumulate enough wealth from this still lucrative fishing and shipping trade to become vessel owners and merchants themselves. Still, like most West Country merchants, they preferred to maintain their home and business premises in England, only venturing to Caplin Bay (now Calvert) and Ferryland seasonally for the fishery. There were a number of Morry men involved in this enterprise, but the one who finally decided to pull up stakes, after the death of his first wife, and move the younger members of his family and his business to Newfoundland was Howard Leopold Morry's great, great grandfather, Matthew.

Matthew Morry and Company set up shop in Caplin Bay in 1784, occupying a grant for a shipping room obtained from the governor, John Campbell. The space they occupied there was expanded in 1790 by a further grant from surrogate magistrate Jacob Waller, Captain of the HMS Rose, and the business continued to develop and expand rapidly from those beginnings.

Matthew Morry chose Caplin Bay rather than Ferryland to settle because all of the best fishing rooms in Ferryland had already been granted or claimed by others. Although there were habitations at Caplin Bay, Matthew was able to obtain a grant for a fishing room from the governor based on the area being unoccupied for forty years or more. This was attested to by Robert Carter in Ferryland, who had been in Newfoundland since about 1750 and who would later become Matthew's father-in-law. It was only two generations later that the Morrys moved to Ferryland.

Initially at least, Matthew was no doubt viewed as somewhat of a carpetbagger or nouveau-riche by the well-established businessmen on the Southern Shore, such as the Carters, Sweetlands, and Windsors. But with his strong business ties to England and a number of eligible sons and daughters coming along, it wasn't long before alliances, marital and business, were forged and the family assumed its place in Newfoundland society. Of course connections with mother England were not completely severed, and for at least two generations afterwards, children were sent off to England to obtain a proper education and marriages and business partnerships were arranged with suitable families in England as well as the "better class" of society in Newfoundland. It was Matthew Morry's grandson, John Henry Morry (Dad Morry's grandfather), who, along with his business partner and brother-in-law, Peter Paint LeMessurier, purchased the Holdsworth House, land and waterside premises in Ferryland, leading to a general refocusing of the family's interests in that area. This was a turning point in the history of the Southern Shore as it represented a final withdrawal of the old guard West Country absentee merchants from Newfoundland.

The first generation of Morry men born in Newfoundland were a privileged and perhaps somewhat spoiled lot. Tales are rife of their adventures, some noble and some not quite so noble. They were involved in managing the family businesses, all related to the fishery

Portrait of John Henry Morry, 1818-1897, Howard Morry's grandfather.

The Holdsworth House, purchased by John Henry Morry, 1844.

and the trade associated with it, but some were also sea captains and agents for other well-known West Country merchants, such as the Newmans.

The sense of privilege that allowed the young men of the family to take on adventures not possible for the average young man in the village extended into the next generations as well. Howard Leopold Morry's father, Thomas Graham Morry, chose to leave his duties as an only son, who should rightly have taken on the family business, to strike out on adventures. He travelled to Montreal in order to enlist in the Provisional Battalion of Infantry (PBI) of the Active Militia of Canada on November 12, 1872. What compelled him to join up was partly a sense of adventure but also the practical possibility of acquiring a land warrant for 360 acres of prime Canadian farmland as his reward for service. While his family was now well established in business in Newfoundland, things were not what they used to be, and downturns in the fishery and the economy had taken their toll on the family fortunes. Thus, examining other possibilities such as this one held some appeal, even for a man whose family had been so closely associated with the sea for many generations.

The so-called Northwest Regiment then being assembled was intended to break up the resistance to Canadian unity being mounted by Louis Riel and his followers in what would become Manitoba and

Saskatchewan (the so-called Northwest Rebellion). In November 1874, at the end of his enlistment, Thomas Graham published his reminiscences of these events in a monograph entitled *From Montreal to Fort Garry: Journal of a Private in Third Expedition.*

Thomas Graham was now nearly twenty-five years old, and he had a decision to make. Would he accept his reward for service of 360 acres of prime farmland in the territory that is now Manitoba, or would he return to Newfoundland to assume his filial duties as his family's eldest and only living son and take over the fishing and shipping enterprises from his father. As it happens, the decision was made for him. His request for his grant of land was lost in the already existing bureaucracy in Ottawa and, as a result, his application missed the deadline and was denied.

Thus, the ongoing tradition of a Morry run fishing and shipping enterprise on the Southern Shore of Newfoundland was guaranteed continued existence for one more generation at least. During that ninety-year period, covering three generations, through ups and downs, the enterprise had grown in value and range of activities, and members of the family had taken on roles in public service as stipendiary magistrates, commissioners of roads and schools, and in almost every other facet of public and private endeavour. They were now among the leading families in Newfoundland and no longer had need of the "mother's apron string" ties that they had

Thomas Graham Morry, right, in Fort Garry during the Northwest Rebellion.

sustained with Britain in the early years. But as we will see, the times and the vagaries of the fragile finances of the colony were to soon threaten that continuity once again.

Howard Leopold Morry's Youth

In his memoirs, Howard recalls the times as being generally good when he was growing up. But a number of significant events, with wide ranging ramifications for Newfoundland society, were to change all that. Here is Dad Morry's summary of his life leading up to these significant events in the early 1890s that changed life forever in the village of Ferryland:

> Well, I had a very happy childhood. All our childhood days, the times were very good, the supplying system was in being then: if a man gave all the fish he got, the merchant would see him through the winter. That is, if he was an honest man, and worked hard, and gave in all his fish. The fishermen of that time were a hardy and happy lot as a rule, and at Christmas, when they all got their jars home from St. John's, then all during Christmas Holidays they would all visit each other's homes and drink and sing and dance, and fight occasionally.

There is a precept in economics that family business dynasties generally tend to decline in the third generation. Whether because of that "natural" law, or because of a number of economic downturns that affected most people in Newfoundland (failures of the fishery, bank collapses, political and sectarian upheaval), it is true that by the time Howard Leopold Morry's father, Thomas Graham Morry, finally assumed the reins of the family enterprises, their status was not what it once had been. While the family still enjoyed the benefits of large tracts of land accumulated over the years, as well as fishing premises and rooms along the shore, and still employed many household and business servants and labourers to minister to their needs, their fortunes were already waning by the time of the great bank crash in 1894, which wiped out many fortunes in Newfoundland, Thomas Graham Morry's included. Howard was only nine at the time and probably had no idea why their lives had changed so drastically all of a sudden. Nor could he imagine the impact that this one event would have on the privileged life that he and his siblings enjoyed. A passage from a letter that he wrote late in life to his daughter, Jean, gives some sense of how privileged indeed that life had been and how suddenly and dramatically all of that changed:

> I remember going to watch a football match on the downs. It was the first time I had seen a football and I sure was scared. And I remember well I had a lovely velvet suit, with silver buttons down the front of it and buttons on the side of the legs and my first pair of braces. In my fright I messed it. Mom was very embarrassed before all the folk.
>
> Next thing in December '94 we were sliding in the middle lane and McFarrell came down the lane with a telegram from Father who was in St John's saying the Banks commercial and businesses were broke. We did not understand then, but we soon found out that it would make quite a difference to us. At that time my Father carried on a big business. Imported all his own goods and had all the money in Bank Notes, as at that time it was the custom to settle in the Fall and Spring. The banks paid five cents on the dollar and he was broke almost. But to finish it the next fall, he had about $10,000 worth of fish and oil going

down to St. John's and as 'twas only a few hours run, to save
money, he neglected to insure it. She was lost with all hands and
that finished him. As far as business was concerned, instead of
declaring insolvent he kept trying to pay his debts and worked
like a slave and all us boys as well.

Thomas Graham Morry was a straight-laced Protestant who neither smoked, nor drank, nor cursed, and there was no way a proud man such as this would settle his debts for 5 cents on the dollar, as most other merchants managed to do. Instead he worked the remainder of his life for the banks, paying off every cent of his debt from the income that otherwise would have provided a comfortable living for his family. And of course his sons felt the brunt of his personal morality as well. Not for them was the luxury of an English education. Even before they were finished whatever schooling was available in the village, they were put to work in the family businesses—without salary. Again, some of Dad Morry's reminiscences to his daughter, Jean, help to explain just how difficult their life had

Catherine and Thomas Morry with Trix, Bert, Howard, and Graham,
ca. 1892.

become, and these recollections also reveal that it was no lie when he recorded his profession as "fisherman" on his attestation papers, for after the crash, that was indeed one of his several jobs:

We set barrels of potatoes and bushels of turnips and we boys had to dig and weed and watch them. Not much play I can tell you. I remember I used to cry because the clay used to dry up my hands and crack them. We got very little time to play. About 1894 he started canning lobsters. Then we really had to work. Get rocks to ballast them and put them in the pots right. If not we'd have to do it all over again. Father hired a hardy boy and he set his traps all around outside the harbour and over in Calvert. My brother Bert and I had 35 traps to haul and bait every morning before school. I was up early—early to bed, early to rise—and then I can tell you in the long Spring mornings, we got up in the cold and frost of the year in early May. After there was frost on the water, I still can feel the cold. Wet sleeves from putting our hands in to change the bait and take out the lobsters. Then I got Water Whelps. You know what they were like, Jean? Both my arms would be covered with small pussie pimples. I had hairy arms; baby arms the fishermen called them. When I was older, I often had boils from the poison in the water.

It must be remembered that these boys were not even teenagers when these events took place. Difficult as it must have been for them at the time, it cannot be overlooked that facing adversity such as this would have hardened them and made Howard more capable of standing up to the rigours that would later face him in Gallipoli and France.

This went on until Howard and his older brother, Bert, would stand it no longer. They schemed to put aside a few dollars each. Enough to afford passage on the train to Western Canada, where they heard men were needed to harvest wheat. They had budgeted enough for the train but not for food along the way and nearly starved but for the charity of strangers en route. The next year, off Dad Morry went again with his brother, Bert, to the Pacific Coast.

I can remember well the morning we left. 'Twas the latter part of July. My brother Bert, Jack Brien and I, we went on the mail carrier's wagon to St. John's. I can see my Father and Mother standing by the gate waving us goodbye and both of them crying.

There were 25 of us put on board a train for a place called Brookdale [Manitoba]. I hired to a fellow called Babb for $2.00 a day and board. Day was from daylight to dark. Well, he started us on a 640 acre farm, that is a mile each way and we

Howard Morry, standing second from left. Howard's mother and father, standing to the right. Graham Morry, seated center of front row, Trix Morry, seated right, ca. 1900.

started one each way. Stooping, that is standing the sheaves up in piles for to be brought to the threshing machine. 'Twas hard work for us and hot, we being used to sea breezes. We met on the far end of the field a few times a day. We started off at breakfast with porridge and fried pork. At noon we got cold pork and bread and beer, for supper, fried pork and pancakes. The water was bad and we being hot and thirsty drank a lot of it and got the back door trots pretty bad.

Well, we worked till the last of November, then came home. My brother got off in Montreal and stayed there. I came on alone, got in St. John's by train, arrived at 7 p.m. and went down to Goodridge Wharf to see if there were any schooners ready for home. My first time away and how glad I was when I went in. My father and mother were sitting before the fire. How glad were they. I had $135.00 I brought home. I gave him $100.00, kept the $35.00 for myself to do me for six months.

Work in the wheat fields was much more difficult than they imagined, and it was work unlike that to which they were accustomed. They stuck it out for one season before giving up. Bert stayed on in Montreal, evidently not able to face the drudgery without pay that awaited them back home. The following year, the two brothers decided to head to BC to hopefully find work in the salmon fishery, something more familiar to them.

Went lobster fishing and boiling oil with my father that summer. We made about $3,500.00 boiling oil and it took it all to pay his old bank crash debts. I never said anything. He was just too honest; we made $110.00 lobster catching, they were scarce. I brought down the lobsters, sold them. Bought a ticket to Victoria, B.C, for $105.00, had $5.00 for food for a train trip across Canada. Nothing for anything else (faith - unafraid). My brother Bert met me at the station in Montreal and came along. I did not know him, he was thin and pale. The last time I'd seen him he was as brown as a berry and very fat. Montreal did not

*agree with him. He had a few dollars more than his passage so
we were all set for the Pacific Coast. He got very sick on the train
and was lifted off the boat in Victoria three days afterward on a
stretcher and brought to the hospital.*

*I did not have a cent left, nor did he. However, friends of my
father, a Mr. and Mrs. Lester of St. John's, took him in and got a
doctor for him as soon as we landed, which was a grand thing
for him, and a very generous and kind deed for these people,
to take a stranger into their home, not knowing what he was
suffering from.*

In his memoirs, Howard tells of the many different kinds of work
that he and his brother, Bert, took on in order to make ends meet on
the west coast. These tales are unfortunately too lengthy to repeat
in their entirety here, a great pity because they make fascinating
reading. But some of his adventures can be repeated in brief:

*As soon as my brother was taken to hospital, I got my grip and
thought I'd look for a cousin of my father's there. And as I was
going up the wharf, I saw a sign, "seaman wanted." So I went in to
the office and signed on for fifty a month. Well, less than an hour
after landing in Victoria, I slung my grip aboard a steamer, the
Princess Victoria and shipped on her as a deck hand. That was
in July 1902. She ran the triangular run; Victoria, Vancouver
and Seattle, about four hours between each place. The crew
had to handle the freight as well and we did not get very much
rest. I asked leave for an hour to go and see my brother, but the
captain would not grant it. I had been on her a week then and
thought I was quite a sailor, so when I did not get leave, I went
up to the office on the wharf, drew a week's pay, and got one of
the sailors to pitch my grip ashore when none of the officers were
looking. So ended my first voyage as a sailor.*

*I never got a chance to see Bert, though I rang him and found
he was improving. He had Typhoid Fever. So I thought I'd get a
job on shore. And I did. A dandy. Working putting in a water*

system in Victoria. Pick and shovel. I always remember the first day I went to work. It was the 9th day of August. The foreman measured off on the pavement each man's work. A strip 2½ feet wide, 29 feet long and 4 feet deep. You did not have much time for looking around especially when you had to dig six inches of concrete off the top. It was very hot, and though we only worked eight hours a day, I was tired at the end of the day.

I used to go to the doss houses at first but my money gave out. You'd pay a quarter, there was a chair two planks for a bed. Just room for the chairs and the bed. They were boarded about five feet up and if you were foolish enough to leave your clothes on the back of a chair, or hang them up; they'd be stolen during the night. Lovely! I slept in one a whole month in Vancouver.

I worked at the job till late in the fall, getting $2.50 a day, but having to pay Bert's board and my own, when work closed down, I was pretty near broke, so I went in search of other work. I worked carrying the hod, building fences, longshore work, digging gardens and wells and all kinds of work you could think of. We used to saw birch for the government institutions for three hours for a meal of scraps. All the hotels and doss houses would send their pig swill out to us—hunger is the best sauce. There was no good help for the poor at that time.

We had to tighten our belts. Once we were down to a meal a day. One meal a day is not much to go on. All these months I could have gone to Victoria and lived with my brother or cousins, but I didn't have $2.50 to pay my passage. And as my boots were gone I bought a second hand pair for $1.50. My brother and I got work to put a fence around the Catholic Church grounds. We made thirty dollars on it, so we built a little shack on the lot we had bought on the instalment plan on Shakespeare Street. And after that, we could live for nine dollars a month each by cutting our fire wood and buying at the cheapest places. We did all kinds of odd jobs putting up fences, digging gardens, liming, etc.

I was always trying to get on the boats again, but could not, as there was a slump on and those that had jobs were holding them.

Then I got a job unloading a big ship and got $23.00 on one shift longshoring. I was tired, having worked over 40 hours straight, but had secured money enough to keep us for almost three months, and by that time, we hoped there would be lots of work.

I sawed wood for the Metropolitan Church for thirty days and paid it all out for board. I made about one dollar a day on an average. 'Twas getting near spring and I quit to go to sea. Went on a tow boat, towing logs down the coast for a month

Howard Leopold Morry in St. John's, ca. 1903.

for thirty a month. When that was over, back to Vic again. No work at anything. I decided to join the army.

Went out to the barracks at Esquimalt. The gate was open and I walked in. Got about 10 yards and was halted and a fellow asked me what I was doing there. I never told him and, as I was going out through the gate, I picked up a quarter. Just enough to get me back to Vic on the street car.

On the way back, sat beside a man. Got in talk with him and he said you're Newfie aren't you? I said yes. He said what in hell are you doing five miles away from the water. I told him. Why, he said, I want a man to count fish and work around a salmon cannery. So I hired on with him at once. Fifty a month and board and fifty cents an hour overtime. So that suited me fine.

I was off next day on the cannery boat to River Inlet. Boy was I delighted. There were about 60 Chinese at this cannery, 80 Japanese, 15 Finlanders, 5 Hindus, and about 300 Nootka Indians. There were 7 white men there. I went there in April, and stayed until September. When it closed down, I had managed to save quite a bit of money. I had a nice time there, and enjoyed the place very much.

I worked in Vancouver next winter and spent most of my Sundays and holidays in Stanley Park. There was a tree there so big that it had a wagon road cut through the centre of it, and enough wood left on each side to keep it standing there for years. I know it is still standing and it is over thirty years since I saw it.

Victoria was a lovely place to live, and I had always intended to go back there and live, but the war put a kink in my plans. The people there were very nice, mostly of Scottish and English descent. I had a great many friends among them, especially among the Scotch, which was rather queer, since my own people were of English descent, except my mother's mother who was of Irish extraction.

I worked in a logging camp up there for a while. The pay was very good, with fellows getting $7.00 for an eight-hour day. Hook tenders and donkey men also got $7.00, while swampers, muckers and snipers got $3.50. I was of the latter class—all we did was round off the butts of the big sticks so that they would not stick in the ground when the donkey was towing them with a steel line.

Our good luck seemed to have petered out again. Bert took a contract to remove a large oak from the front of a man's residence. We were three days at it, from day to dark, and had spoiled three axes with stones that grew up in the roots of the tree. Then, when we thought we had the worst over and would finish on the morrow and make about fifty dollars, a gale of wind came that night and blew it in on the house. Result, $100 damages and a fortnight's work for us with no pay. The next I got a nail up through my foot and lost three month's work, but it could have been worse, for I got $10 a week from the Forester Society that I was a member of. Then Bert got laid off, or could not get a contract.

As soon as I got well, I started off in the country one day to visit a cousin. I took my revolver, a .32, with me, as I thought

I might get a shot at pheasants, and so I did. About two miles from town, I saw a pheasant and made a grab for the revolver, and set her off in my pocket. Result, a bullet through the shin bone. I didn't feel any pain at first, just felt my leg getting weak. So I started to hop back to town, and quite a hop it was. After hopping for about 10 minutes, I hooked my toe under a root and fell. I could not get up, so I crawled the rest of it to the city limits, where a couple of boys saw me and got me home.

I was laid up for three weeks. One night, I woke up in an awful fever and got the doctor, who said "blood poisoning" as soon as he entered the room. I was rushed off to the Jubilee Hospital, and for a long time I was afraid I'd lose my leg, but after three months, I was discharged, broke and unable to work, so it was Bert's turn to keep the home fires burning.

Now my time in Victoria was getting short, and time passes on without waiting for anyone. My brother Graham wanted to come away and I decided to go home for a while and give him a chance. So the war came and I never went back.

Bert could not bring himself to head back to Newfoundland lest their father put him back in reins. So he stayed in BC and later enlisted along with his younger brother, Graham, in the Canadian Army when war broke out. Neither of them ever returned home. Bert settled in British Columbia, and Graham eventually immigrated after the war to the "Boston States."

Meantime, Howard had to return to Newfoundland or leave their poor father without a single working-age son to assist him in the business. He headed back to Newfoundland where he was to enlist in the Newfoundland Regiment shortly after the declaration of war by Britain on August 4, 1914.

Newfoundland, Britain's oldest colony, was among the first of the Commonwealth countries to respond. A proclamation was sent out on August 22, 1914, by the Newfoundland Patriotic Association calling for all able-bodied men to come forward and volunteer. They had promised the government they would raise an initial draft of

500. There was a rush to join up, and nearly twice that number had volunteered by the end of September, though many were disqualified when they took their medicals. Howard had to wait until the fishery was done for the year and was too late to make the first 500 but was accepted as Private No. 726 when he signed his attestation papers on December 17, 1914. At the time, he was a fine figure of a man: one half inch under six feet tall and 180 pounds, in perfect health from the hard labour he had endured since boyhood, and a fine specimen for the new Newfoundland Regiment. His only physical impairment was somewhat of an embarrassment to him—the self-inflicted bullet wound to the left shin which he suffered in an accident while working in BC.

Last Years at Home

It is time to let Howard Leopold Morry tell his own story of the war years overseas. The remainder of this book is comprised of sections taken directly from his diaries, with only light editing and annotations to explain certain names and terms that are not self-evident or that may be confusing to the reader. Transcribing these passages from the original diaries has occupied a number of family members over the years. But this is the story of Howard Leopold Morry, as told in his own words, and it is to him that we all owe a debt of gratitude for having taken the time to record these experiences in an unvarnished and honest manner so that we can better understand the privations and misery that he and his fellow Newfoundlanders endured during the war years.

Things were getting kind of dull in Victoria so I decided to go home for a while, and I made arrangements, and bought my ticket, it cost me $103.00. If I had not bought that ticket I wonder what would have happened. I would probably have gone over with the Canadians, I would not have met Fredris, and

wouldn't have the family we have. It's strange what things hap-
pen and alter the course of our lives altogether.

Fishing was good, plenty of work on the fishery, and we had
great times, till the war put an end to it for all time as far as I
was concerned.

Records show that Howard Morry enlisted, or at least signed his attestation paper, on December 17, 1914. It would appear that he was already committed to join up in some manner as early as November of that year, but had been given leave until this date, presumably to tidy up his personal affairs prior to reporting. It is a curious fact that, in none of the four separate versions of his war memoirs, Howard never mentions the circumstances or timing of his actual enlistment.

A full copy of his service records, including his attestation paper, as well as those for all the members of the Royal Newfoundland Regiment, are available on microfilm at The Rooms (Provincial Archives Division). These records are gradually being digitised and made freely available online. The originals are held at the National Archives in Ottawa.

Many of Howard's best friends and cousins from Ferryland and the surrounding areas had already enlisted or were about to do so at the same time he did. These included friends and hunting partners like Jack Barnable, Jack Devereaux, and Stan Winsor. To say goodbye to the place they loved, to which many would not return, Howard and these men went hunting and returned late the night before they were to report for duty, perhaps reluctant to leave this good life behind.

When I got home [late the last night before leaving] *poor father*
and mother were waiting up for me, and though I knew they
felt hurt they never said a word or did I. We sat and talked till
almost daylight. Then to bed. That last night at home before the
war, I slept like a log, though when Reg [Howard's son] *joined*
the Navy [in wwii] *he and I slept together and we talked far*

Howard Morry (centre) in 1912 with two friends, Jack Devereaux (left) and Stan Winsor (right). Jack and Stan were L/Cpl. and Cpl. in the RNR, respectively. Jack died of injuries sustained in the war on April 17, 1920.

John Joseph (Jack) Barnable in uniform with Howard's younger brother, John, and after the war on crutches. Jack initially joined the Royal Naval Reserve but transferred to the Royal Newfoundland Regiment to be with more of his pals. He survived the war but lost a foot and part of his left leg, which gave him trouble ever after. He died in 1925.

Howard Leopold Morry (marked with an X) in Standard Regimental Platoon Photograph, ca. 1915. Inconsistencies in uniforms reveal this photo was taken in St. John's before departure.

(L) *Howard Leopold Morry and a fellow recruit in St. John's, winter 1914-15.* (R) *A staged photograph before leaving St. John's. The photo is curious for two reasons. First, Howard Morry, who was six feet tall, was the tallest man in every other photo taken of him with other soldiers. Second, the tall man beside him, Captain Marcus C. Sorensen of the Hawk, who must be at least six feet, six inches tall, is wearing a uniform that is not typical of a merchant seaman's garb. This is a bit of a mystery.*

into the night. I was wondering and thinking of what he'd see and do before we'd meet again if ever, and that is what advancing years do; they make you think. It's grand to be young, once anyway and play your part among men for a while.

Early Training (and Courting)
in Edinburgh

H oward enlisted in what would become "C" Company of the Newfoundland Regiment (it was initially labelled Number 1 Company, Reserve Force). On his attestation paper, under profession, he noted "fisherman" and declared an annual salary of $400, a decent wage for those days. A distant relation of Howard's, Col. Thomas Skinner, had formed the original Newfoundland Regiment in 1795 though it is doubtful Howard was aware of that fact at the time. Almost none of the enlistees would

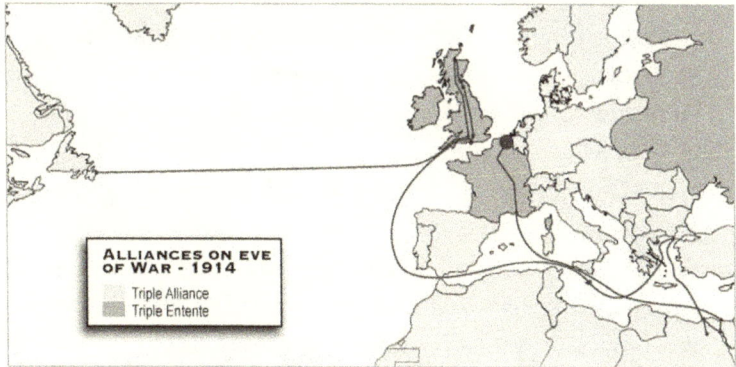

ALLIANCES ON EVE
OF WAR - 1914

Triple Alliance
Triple Entente

The "Trail of the Caribou." This map shows the route followed by the Royal Newfoundland Regiment from the time they left home until the end of the war.

have had any formal military training though many of them were recruited from groups like the Anglican Church Lads' Brigade, the Catholic Cadet Corps, the Methodist Guards, and the Presbyterian Newfoundland Highlanders. These paramilitary denominational groups had some training in drill and discipline but were hardly professional soldiers. Urgent training was needed and was commenced before embarking for Britain, where training in earnest took place.

August 3, 1957

Today I read a book on Gallipoli by Alan Morehead. I noticed in his book that he said that the troops that fought in Gallipoli did not fight in France, which is not true. The 29th Division, which we were in, went to France and fought in France and Belgium. Another thing, he never once mentioned the Newfoundland Regiment, and we were in both evacuations and were among the very last men off both Suvla and Cape Hellas. We came off Gallipoli 350 strong. I believe we had lost a lot of men with dysentery and jaundice and fever of different kinds, besides those killed and wounded.

I've often thought of trying to remember some of my experiences and the boys of our own 11 platoon, C company, especially. There in the trenches we could not move anywhere as we had only a couple of miles strip on the coast and were continually under shellfire and rifle fire as well. So we could not tell much of what the other buddies did.

Well to continue with my story. We trained in St. John's till the fifth of February, 1915 and then one fine morning we boarded the old steamer Neptune, *and cut our way about twenty miles through the ice, out to a large steamer called the* Dominion *that was waiting for us. It had been very frosty for about a week before we left and even out there, we could walk on boarding quite well. In memory I still can see the crowd on the wharf,*

(T) *Howard Morry's platoon in "C" Company. Howard is the tall man in the middle of the back row.* (B) *Howard (third from right) and other recruits and well-wishers in St. John's before boarding.*

EARLY TRAINING (AND COURTING) IN EDINBURGH 27

women trying to get a last hand shake and goodbye kiss from their sons, and sweethearts waving goodbye, and the fathers and brothers cheering the departing ones and trying to keep up a brave front. And so good old C Company set sail and we were off on the great adventure. The hardest was over, and now we had the war and its great trials ahead of us. It's good we couldn't see what fate had in store for us, and the words of one old verse come to me, "We went away boys and came back scornful men, who had diced with death under the blazing skies".

We had a very pleasant passage across, though when we got near the Irish coast the submarines had us uneasy, but the Captain got us in safely. It was very foggy when we arrived at Liverpool and we could hear steamers rushing past us in the fog, hear the bells ringing on them, and men talking; it was a strange thing

The Neptune *boarding members of the* RNR *in St. John's harbour. Howard Morry expressed the views of all Newfoundland volunteers in a caption he wrote on the back of this photograph: "This is the ship* Neptune *that we left St. John's for overseas on, Feb. 5, 1915. 'C' Company, Royal Newfoundland Regiment on the 'Great Adventure'—the fight for the freedom of the world. H. Morry Regt. # 726 Royal Newfoundland Regiment".*

to us. At length we landed in Liverpool. A cheering, laughing, carefree bunch, we were given a great reception by the people on the wharf.

Then we entrained for Edinburgh, where we were billeted in the Castle. After a couple of days in the Castle we were taken out for a route march one day and the kids began calling out to us about our bonnets. So we were brought back again, and kept in the Castle till we got new uniforms and caps, puttees, etc. The ones we got at home were the first made in the

Howard Leopold Morry (marked "Dad") and mates on leave in Edinburgh after they received their standard-issue caps.

country and should have been the last as they were scandalous.

Well at last the happy day came and we were allowed out around the city to see the sights and meet the kind people of this grand city. We soon made friends and were invited everywhere. The Castle itself is worth a trip overseas to see, with all its history and objects of historical value: the crown room, with its crown jewels; the reception room with its suits of armour, etc.; Queen Margaret's chapel; Mons Meg, a big gun taken from Germany hundreds of years ago; the dungeons under the Castle where great men were imprisoned and spent many years in solitary confinement. Then from there to Holy Rood Palace, with Queen Mary's room, just as it was when she lived in it; the place where Rizzio was slain, etc. Arthur's Seat, Queen Margaret's Loch, the Braid Hill, Loughton Park, the Meadows, the Princes St. Garden, the loveliest place I ever saw. Then there were trips around to country places, quiet lanes and avenues all near Edinburgh. Colinton Dell, Mussel Borough, the Forth Bridge, the Dean Bridge and a thousand more places of interest around there where we visited and spent many happy hours with our Scottish friends. And to us Newfoundlanders who were used to the hard and lonely life of the outports it was a great and wonderful city and the most of us when we went to the front always looked back to Edinburgh as our second home.

In this phase of the memoir's narrative and both before and afterwards, Howard Morry spends little time explaining what training the raw troops of the RNR received. Other sources are more fulsome in this regard. I suspect that, as this entire narrative gives testament, Howard was not a model soldier and had little use for the military discipline expected of soldiers in training. That independent streak, though not unique amongst the soldiers of the RNR by any means, was undoubtedly accentuated in his case by his more mature age and the fact that many of the NCOs and officers from whom he would have been receiving orders were not only his juniors chronologically but also much less experienced in the ways of the world.

From other sources we learn that the training in St. John's prior to embarking was little more than marching drill. They were even initially forced to use makeshift weapons since there were precious few real weapons available, and they did not receive these before they embarked. There is also mention made of some riflery drill on the Southside hills, but for most of the men from outside of St. John's this would have been superfluous, as they already knew their way around a rifle and how to use it.

No doubt the young troops were given their initial introduction to the "Kings Regs," though they appeared to have had little impact on Howard and many of his companions. The *Kings Regulations and Orders for the Army* were a statement of the code of conduct and military discipline expected of all British soldiers, including those from the colonies and dominions. The full document was in fact a lengthy (over 400 pages), hard-covered book, containing nearly 2000 detailed clauses or "paragraphs," but an abbreviated version of the most common infractions and the associated punishment was carried by all officers and read out to the troops, assembled and standing at attention, when a serious misconduct of the company as a whole or a squad within the company had taken place.

Once in Scotland, however, and especially after their arrival at Stobs Camp, their training became much more real. First of all, they were under the watchful eye of battle-hardened, professional NCOs from the British Army, many of whom had experience in India and South Africa. While daily route marches were still the order of the day, primarily to build stamina, training now included the use of military equipment such as bombs (hand grenades) and machine guns that none of these recruits would have ever seen before, let alone used. They were also taught the use of the bayonet in close combat, knowledge they would unfortunately need all too soon. In addition, they were given instruction to some degree in military strategy associated with

How a Soldier should get his Pay.

1. The Paymaster of your regiment keeps an account of the pay you earn from the time you join as a recruit. The money is paid to you by the captain of your company or other officer under whom you serve. He informs the paymaster how much he pays you, so that the paymaster always knows how much is due to you.

2. When you join as a Recruit the recruiting officer pays you.

3. When you go to the Depot, and from there to your Battalion, Regiment, Battery, or Company, your captain pays you every week.

4. When you go on furlough you get an advance of pay from your captain.

5. When you are in Hospital you are not allowed to have money. Stamps, writing materials, &c., will be obtained from the medical officer.

6. If you are sent on sick furlough from the hospital, and your company is in this country, you should write to your captain, if possible three or four days before you leave the hospital. Ask him to send some money to the hospital to be given to you on leaving, and send him your furlough address, so that he may send on the remainder of the pay due to you when you have been invalided home from Active Service, see para. 8.

7. When abroad on Active Service you get your money from your captain or other officer under whom you happen to be serving. When you embark a little Pay Book is given you in which the officer who pays you enters the amount. You keep this

book all the time you are abroad, so you always know how much you have to come to you.

8. If you return home from Active Service, sick or wounded, your captain cannot pay you, but:
   (a) If you are going on sick furlough, write to your paymaster, some days before you go, if possible, stating your regimental number, rank, name, company, regiment or corps, and your furlough address, and ask him to send you your money.
   (b) The medical officer of the hospital will give you an advance on leaving.

9. If you are in hospital, having come home sick or wounded, and you wish some of your money sent to a relative, write to your paymaster stating the amount and the name and address of the person to whom you wish it sent.

10. When you are discharged from the Army you get the balance due to you from your captain. If not settled with when you go, send him your address and ask for your balance. If you think you have not been paid all the money due to you write to your paymaster. But if you have come home from abroad and have been discharged from the Army on leaving the hospital, write to your paymaster for your balance.

NOTES.

11. When you write to the paymaster or your captain don't forget to state your regimental number, rank, name, company and corps.

12. Write to your captain, not to the pay serjeant. Don't write to the War Office until you have tried the right person—your captain or paymaster.

13. Any officer or serjeant can tell you the address of your paymaster.

KEEP THIS.

Instructions on how to get paid. It is difficult to imagine that a soldier needed written instructions on how to get his pay. Somewhat of an excess of information, typical of military bureaucracies through the ages.

DIRECTIONS FOR USE & CARE OF TUBE HELMETS

DESCRIPTION.
These Helmets are the same as the "Smoke Helmet" already issued, except that stronger chemicals are added and a "Tube-valve" provided through which to breathe out. The Tube-valve makes helmet cooler and saves the chemicals from being affected by breath.
N.B. Wearer cannot breathe in through the Tube-valve, this is intended for breathing out only.

DIRECTIONS FOR USE.
Remove **Service Cap.** Pull helmet over head. Adjust so that goggles are opposite eyes. Tuck in skirt of helmet under coat collar and button coat so as to close in skirt of helmet. Hold the "Tube" lightly in lips or teeth like stem of pipe, so as to be able to breathe in past it and out through it.
Breathe in through mouth and nose, using the air inside the helmet. Breathe out through tube only.

DIRECTIONS FOR CARE OF TUBE-HELMET.
(1) *Do not remove the Helmet from its Waterproof Case except to use for protection against Gas.*
(2) *Never use your Tube-Helmet for practice or drill. Special helmets are kept in each Company for instruction only.*

WITHDRAW THESE INSTRUCTIONS FROM THE CASE AND KEEP FOLDED IN YOUR PAY BOOK.

Instructions for use and care of tube helmets.

the kind of trench warfare they were to face on the Peninsula and in France and Belgium.

This training would have continued once they were relocated to the south of England near the point of embarkation, but by then the methods would have been second nature to them, and the more important lessons learned there would have had to do with landing procedures once they reached Gallipoli.

Training in Egypt, mainly route marches once again, was brutal, due to the intense heat, and it was intended to be so because, at least initially, these were the conditions the men would face on the Peninsula, and almost none of them had any experience in coping with such conditions.

If they didn't know it already, there were at least three things that the soldiers of the Royal Newfoundland Regiment would be taught as part of their basic training in Scotland, and it is a toss-up as to which was the most important to them: how to get their pay, how to use their gas masks, and how to mooch some "fags."

The standard issue gas mask for Newfoundland troops, also used by other allied troops at the beginning of the war, was invented by a Newfoundlander, Dr. Cluny MacPherson. They were better than breathing through a damp piece of cloth, which was the initial technique recommended to combat chlorine and mustard gas, but they were also uncomfortable and difficult to use and were soon replaced with improved equipment.

Despite the training and red tape, Dad Morry always held fond memories of Edinburgh.

These people seemed to have taken us right in to their hearts and would not let anything be said to us even when some of our lads, in pure exuberance of spirits, would start a row for the pure

An insert from a *"package of fags."* Here called *"fags,"* cigarettes were also known as *"Mayo's"* after the Mayo tobacco that Francis Thomas (Mayo) Lind, an RNR enlisted man and scribe who wrote extensively for the newspapers, petitioned successfully to have shipped to the troops to raise morale.

devilment of it. And many is the paragraph that appeared in the Edinburgh papers making excuses for our bad deeds. We also went to the Picture Gallery, Shakespeare Monument, Scotland's Folly, all the theatres and picture houses, and must say that the three months I spent in Edinburgh were the happiest and most enjoyable of my whole life.

March passed along pretty quickly, and then on the first day of April, 1915, I was sitting in the barrack room at Edinburgh Castle, writing home, when Mont came in and said, "are you going out tonight." I said, "I'll probably go by and by."

Private Howard Leopold Morry, "C" Company, RNR, in Edinburgh shortly after arrival at the same time wedding photographs were taken on June 3, 2015.

This was Howard's cousin, Wilfred Montgomery Windsor of Aquaforte, who was his companion in arms through the events of Gallipoli and on into the first part of their time at the Somme. Although Mont was invalided due to jaundice before Beaumont-Hamel, he was able to make a full enough recovery to stay on in Britain, serving in both the RNR and the Newfoundland Forestry Corps and attaining the rank of CQMS—Company Quarter Master Sergeant.

He said, "come out with me and meet a nice girl." He said, "a chum of mine wanted to come but he was on picket duty," and I thought, well it's too bad to disappoint the Lassie, I'll go. And, as she hadn't met the other chap, there was no harm done. We were to dine at Fairley's Restaurant on Leith Street and then go to the pictures or the last show at the Empire Theatre. It's funny how simple things alter the course of your whole life.

Fredris Minty (right) with her sister, Mary, in Edinburgh, ca. April-May, 1915.

Mont and I went to Fairley's to wait for the girls and we went in to have a drink while we were waiting. We were there when I turned around and saw two girls passing us going in to the Dining Hall. Mont was talking to a chap when I said, "here they are Mont" (I'd never seen them before), and sure enough it was them. Mont came along and said, "that's them, I thought you did not know them." I said, "I never saw them before." Love at first sight I guess. Well we were introduced, and so began our short and sweet courtship. Fredris, at that time, was not yet twenty; tall and fair with a lovely complexion, blue laughing eyes. I was captured right away.

That was the first day of April. We were married the second of June. Your mom's birthday [here he is writing to his daughter, Jean] *was the third of April. I gave her a present of a silver Caribou Head Broach that was for sale on Princes Street, the Scot's Jewellers. I guess now that they'd sell a few for chaps and their girlfriends. We went to a show that night and she said she'd meet me next night and, by hook or by crook, I saw her every night that she was out. Well it was such a lovely time for the few weeks we were in Edinburgh till we were moved to Stobs Camp* [in May 1915].

"Two shall be born the whole wide world apart;
And speak in different tongues and have no thought
Each of the other's being, and no heed;
And these o'er unknown seas to unknown lands
Shall cross, escaping wreck, defying death,
And all unconsciously shapes every act
And bend each wandering step to this one end, —
That, one day, out of darkness, they shall meet
And read life's meaning in each other's eyes."
[Here Howard quotes "Fate," by Susan Marr Spalding, in
Wings of Icarus (1802).]

I went to see her father and mother and showed them letters of
recommendation as to my character and met the whole family;
and a lovely family they were. I went there many nights during
the weeks that followed and we often paid visits to her married
sister, Alicia's, home, where we had music and sing-songs every
Sunday afternoon and night, and some nights through the week.
It would generally be about 1 a.m. when Mont and I would get
to the Barracks. Mont still went with the girl I first met Fredris
with and, as she lived in the flat below Fredris, we went home
together. And by the generous use of a lot of Whisky and a little
soft soap, we always got by the guard at the gate. Of course our
Sergeant at the Barracks would not post us as missing but mark
us as present at roll call in the evening. He said if we were not in
for roll call in the morning he would have to mark us as missing.
He was a good trump and never changed. His name was Joe
McKinley and he now keeps a garage in St. John's.

We managed to escape detection until one night about a
week before we left Edinburgh for Stobs Camp, when we were
caught out at 2 a.m., four hours after we should have been
in Barracks. So our leave was stopped. That was pretty hard
on me, but the old saying "love defies locksmith" proved true
again. For I found where some of our chaps whose leave was
also stopped had found an open drain pipe which carried water

off the causeway in a big flood, had an outlet on Princes Street Gardens. It would be about a twelve or fourteen inch main and was about forty feet long and then had a drop of eight or ten feet when you got there, before you came to the ground, and besides there was not any way of getting back if you did get out. I took several looks at the pipe in the long Spring evenings when I was barred in, and spent them looking over the wall at all the Lads and Lassies strolling around Princes Street Garden.

I had sent out a couple of notes and got back answers, but there was not much to that and, knowing that we would be leaving Edinburgh for we knew not where, I was getting pretty desperate. I had asked for a pass every evening but was refused. So I decided to go out the drain pipe way even though the chaps that had gotten out that way told me I'd probably get stuck, as they were small fellows and I weighed 212 lbs. Nothing ventured nothing win, was my motto, and the risk did not bother me as much as the thought of getting another sight of Fredris before we left for somewhere.

So I waited until about 9 p.m., went down by the drain pipe, stripped at the mouth of it and rolled up my clothes and put my equipment belt around them, shoved them in the pipe and got in feet first behind them. I found that by putting my hands over my head I had lots of room. The pipe had a drop of about six feet I should think on its forty foot length and I slipped down pretty easily with a little twisting and shoving on spots of rust, etc. whenever I could leverage with my hands. I thought it must be about forty miles long instead of 40 feet. By and by, I went a little quicker and I felt my clothes drop; the next thing I dropped on my hands and knees on the grass with a few little patches of skin off my shoulders and hips.

I got my clothes, got under a tree and dressed, then went to a rest station to get a bath, brushed my clothes and was quite the thing. Arrived at Fredris' just as they came in. My oh my! That will be 25 years ago on the earlier part of March this year. I can remember our meeting yet as plain as if 'twas yesterday.

She forgot to ask me how I got out and I did not tell her, for it's a bad thing to make a girl too wise. And besides I was feeling ashamed of the foolish thing I did, but now looking backward, I think I would do the same thing again. However, that night we agreed to get married on the second day of June.

I wandered back to the Barrack like a man in a trance and, as luck would have it, a great pal of mine was on the gate and, instead of being arrested for being out without a pass, I was let in and got safely to my billet, thanks to my good pal, Davey Carew, who was killed at Gallipoli before he reached his 18th birthday.

I took that escape as a good omen and the next morning we went on a 25 mile route march in full marching order. That meant 70 lbs. of a load, and I can tell you that when the straps of my pack rested on my skinned shoulders, and the belt and trenching tool and water bottle and haversack scraping on my back and hips, it was not a very enjoyable route march for me. However, I stood it OK and they healed quickly, long before the second of June when we were married.

Training at Stobs Camp

When the Newfoundland Regiment was relieved of its garrison duties in Edinburgh Castle, a duty which was in fact deemed to be a great honour for a colonial regiment, they were next sent to Stobs Camp near Hawick, Scotland, on May 11, 1915, for intensive training. Actually they camped at Acreknowe Camp, just a few hundred yards from Stobs. This training was essential because most of the men had only just joined up shortly before departing from Newfoundland, and they lacked any formal military training for the most part. To have sent them into battle in this condition would have been little short of murder.

Howard resumes his story:

What memories, drill every day, the presentation of the colours. We were up there about the first week in May, first pay day, and I applied for a pass for a weekend at Edinburgh and got it. Had a great weekend. Coming back to camp there was not any sentry at the gate. There was a big sign over it with the name Stobs Camp, and a thought came to my mind. I was feeling blue, so I climbed up and wrote "Abandon Hope, All Ye who Enter Here." It was days before any of the officers noticed it. In the meantime, some chap had got a nice square of paste board and printed it in letters about an inch long. There was an enquiry but of course, no one wrote it. A military secret.

I remember once in Stobs Camp, Capt. Donnelly was drilling us. When he dismissed us Mike Downey, from Placentia way, hurried after the Captain and, putting his hand on the Captain's shoulder, he said "Hey Jim, what about a couple of shillings off you for a couple of beer." We all got a great kick out of it. Donnelly read all the King's Regs and threw the book at us next parade.

Next week applied again and was turned down. Next weekend applied for a week off to get married. The Colonel told me I could not get married according to Army Regulations without

(TOP) *Tents of the Newfoundland Regiment at Stobs Camp, Scotland, May 1915.* (BOTTOM) *Presentation of colours to* RNR *at Stobs Camp, June 10, 1915.*

getting a written certificate of the girls character, so that put me in a fix.

Capt. Bernard, who brought me to the Colonel, asked me what I was going to do, so I said, "Well Sir, these people have over a hundred guests invited and all preparations made, there is only one thing for me to do. I'll have to beat it." He was a sport, and said don't do anything rash, and said get back as soon as you can. I said O.K. Sir.

Next day, Friday, was payday. We were to be married on Monday, the second of June. I got Sgt. McKinley to put me on guard duty, so I'd be off duty the next day. I also got him to fix the guard so I'd be off at 4 a.m. He'd get someone to take my place while the guard was being dismissed. Edinburgh was eighty miles away. And at that time there was no other way to get to Edinburgh without paying a lot of money. If I walked I'd be asked for my pass every few miles and, as I had neither one, I'd have been arrested right away. [Note that, in point of fact,

Howard Morry's squad at Stobs Camp, May 28, 1915. Back row: Joachim Murphy, David Stephenson, Willis White, James Joseph (Jim) Gladney, Howard Morry, and Lewis Head. Front row: Ernest (Ernie) Heath, Henry (Harry) Mifflin, Harold James Andrews, Either Robert William Heale or Arthur Heale, and William P. (Bill) Dalton.

he did have a pass, but it was a forged one.] *I decided to risk the train. So in camp the boys had a few shillings collected for me and I said good bye to them and I walked four miles or so on the opposite way from Edinburgh to the next station away from the camp so they would not know where to look for me and bought a ticket for Edinburgh and boarded the* Flying Scotsman *when it came along and got in among a bunch of our fellows, who were going there on a weekend pass, and went to the toilet and closed the door till we were past Stobs. But, I needn't have*

Two forged passes. The second allowed Howard Morry to attend his wedding.

bothered, for the first stop was in Edinburgh. I did not know it, and only by pure chance I got off at the Waverly Station. I was yarning off to a chap and had taken off my tunic and had all my gear on the seat when the train stopped. I thought they said this train's first stop was at Edinburgh. I looked out grabbed my gear and hopped out on the station just in time. I got dressed there and went to 6 Ardmillan Terrace and they were all in bed. As they were expecting me on the regular train in about four hours' time. She took almost three hours from Stobs instead of the Scotsman's one hour.

They were surprised to see me, but scared when they found out I'd broke leave, but that did not bother me in the least. It was getting caught and sent back before I was married that worried me. So the next two days were spent in dodging the Military Police and a good job I made of it. We went to the Theatre and there were two of them in the doorway. I passed them as bold as brass and they never asked to see my pass. Monday morning came and I still had to go buy the wedding ring.

Mont and I went, as Mont had just arrived on pass. We went down to the North Bridges and I just had bought the ring and walked right in to the arms of our Police Sergeant, Walter Greene. He said first show me any kind of a piece of paper will do, the Red Cap Sergeant major is watching me. So I showed him a pass that Harold Andrews had written for me, and forged Captain Bernard's name to it. He laughed when I passed it to him and said beat it, but turn up at the Battalion Headquarters in a day or so as we are soon going to the front. I promised and went off quite happy. I was able to repay him afterwards when he was sick and jaundiced up at Cape Helles. I stole prunes and dates and figs from the English ration dump for him. The Turks used to shell it every evening at dusk. We found that then the guard was withdrawn for a while. Then a few of us moved in and made our haul, from the officer's dump. Found potted ham and chicken and all kinds of goodies. Guess it kept us alive.

I had not got out of Sergeant Greene's sight, before I was stopped by the Scotch Sergeant Major. Your pass he said, quite stiff. I looked up and down the street, not another Newfoundlander in sight, so it was no use for me to sock him as there were dozens of soldiers around but none of our crowd to back me up. So I showed him the old pass again, but he said I'm sorry lad, but there are 350 of your Newfoundlanders away without leave and we got strict orders to round you all up. So I

Two legitimate passes: one issued at Edinburgh Castle and the other at Stobs Camp.

said O.K. I'm going to be married this evening, and the people are put to a big expense and if I'm arrested all will be wasted. He asked who the girl was and I told him and it seems he knew Fredris' father well, and he handed me back the pass and said, keep out of sight of the police, and report as soon as you can. I promised I would and he shook my hand and wished me luck and so ended that episode.

We were married that evening, in a hall two doors away from the house. But, first we had to get a car to pick up Fredris, who was staying at her sisters. When we got to the hall there were about a hundred girlfriends of Fredris' there. I remember while we were standing by the corner windows, there was a column of troops marching past. There was a whole division 16,000 men. We had just got through in time. We had had a nice dance and supper, although the fifteen Newfoundlanders that were invited did not get down, owing to all leave being stopped on account of so many AWOL. We got a bunch of Canadians and managed O.K. and next evening we left for our Honeymoon at a place called Bavelaw Mill, up north.

Next day Fredris and I went to get our photos taken. She'd go ahead and look up and down the street and if there was not any Red Caps in sight, she put her hand up and I'd come on. Then she'd go on again and I'd follow at the signal. Anyway we got to the photographer and back without anything happening. That evening we went to Morningside Station, and again I got a-hide till the train pulled out. Got off at Balerno, where Fredris' Aunt Ellen Hislop had a couple of big farms at Bavelaw Mill, and we stayed there for about eight days, a lovely quiet little place and at that time of the year the hills were all purple with heather. We had a lovely time there, I hated to leave it. We had a dance whilst there. Jim Minty and Jim Stormont came up from Edinburgh. The oldest boy of the family of seven Hislops, was about forty, had an awful squeaky voice and no hair on his face. I said to Jim Stormont, "is he a girl?" And Jim said, "There's doubt laddie, lets away and see." So we got him out for a drink, but he squealed so

Banns and marriage certificate. St. Michael's Presbyterian Church, Edinburgh, June 2, 1915.

much, the crowd came out and it's still a mystery!

But all things must have an end. Well, one evening out we were on the hills and we saw a soldier on a bicycle going up to the door and I was scared to come down. By and by one of the lads came up and said, "There's a soldier to have a crack wi' ye." So we went down, and 'twas Mont. He said the call was out for all defaulters to return to their unit at once. So 'twas over, the happiest week of my life. I knew it was time for me to report back again. So on a lovely spring evening we left Balerno, and went out and took the train for Edinburgh again, back to the world of realities. Back to Edinburgh, spent a day and a night in Edinburgh and then left for Stobs Camp by train, on the following night. A four mile walk from the station. No money for bus fare, raining hard and black as the inside of a cow. Crawled past the sentry, found my tent and in 10 minutes was asleep before Reveille. Fell in with the bunch at 6 a.m. after being away from the Regiment for ten days without leave. But as soon as the Sergeant-Major saw me he fell out a couple of men and put me under arrest. I was marched off to the Guard House and put in a cell.

It was quite dark to me after the bright sunlight. But I heard a voice say "Hello Morry, what are you in for." I told him, and so I found it was Bill Anderson. His father was a bank manager in St. John's. A wild Harum-Scarum chap who had been away for three months masquerading as a Royal Scot officer. He ran bills for £900 I heard afterward, and his father had to pay. He was discharged from the Regiment but joined a Canadian unit, gained distinction and was killed in action. He was a good trump. We had a few drinks in the cell as they had not searched Billy when they put him in and, on the whole, spent a very enjoyable forenoon, swapping experiences etc., and at 2 p.m. we were marched off before the Colonel for trial. There were about fifty there, quite a defaulters parade.

Bill was drunk enough to be cheeky and got six months. I just had a kind

Wedding photograph of Fredris Minty and Howard Leopold Morry.

of cheerful jag and came up with a grin. The Colonel read the charge: "Absent without leave for ten days. What have you to say for yourself?" He said, "remove your cap Private Morry." I was just removing it when the Sgt. Major, an English regular army bully grabbed it off my head. I just turned and gave him a look. The Colonel said, "replace that man's cap." And now he said remove your cap and I did. I just grinned and said "Nothing Sir." Then he said, "Have you any excuse to make or is there anything you wish to say." I answered "No Sir." He looked at me and I could see my finish. I drew 10 days' pay stopped, and ten days I was taken away to the guard tent to answer the defaulter's call every 1/2 hour when not doing pioneer duty or pack drill.

Pioneer duty was cleaning out the latrines and emptying slops, scrubbing floors etc. Pack drill is, or was, being drilled in full marching order, that is pack containing oil sheet, overcoat, change of underwear, shaving gear, etc., also your rifle, 250 rounds of ammunition, entrenching tool, etc.; in all weighing 75 lbs. The drill sergeant would get the squad to be drilled and take them out to some quiet place where there is lots of room and, if he was a tough guy, he could make it pretty tough for you, because he could stand and give the order and make you double for say 100 yds., then blow the whistle and point in another direction, and if you got stubborn he'd keep you at it for hours. However the bunch I drilled with the final three days were gritty and fair minded enough to know that we were getting what we deserved, and we took it all with a smile and, he being a good trump, let us off easy, when there wasn't any officer around. The worst part of all was after we came into the guard tent. At 5 p.m. you'd have to answer the defaulters call every half hour from that to nine o'clock, and as there was quite a roll call of defaulters when I was on, sometimes we'd only be about ten minutes or so in camp when we'd have to eat and run to answer our names again. That defaulter's call rang in our ears for weeks afterward.

However time passes and at last I was free and the next pay day was a blank to me; also the next one wasn't a very good one, but my chums were good. On the next payday I asked for leave again and to my surprise was granted it, although a soldier was not to get leave for at least thirty days after defaulting.

So I got a pass and went off to Edinburgh for the weekend. I often think how quickly these weekends passed. Almost like a flash, we got paid Friday, grabbed a train for Edinburgh, and had to be back in time for drill on Monday. It was fine going, but coming back to camp was another thing. But after all, it was all great; even coming back to the boys again had its bright side: the gossip of the camp, a few drinks of beer with congenial companions and lots of other things that make a soldier's life exciting and interesting.

So another week passed almost and on Thursday came a telegram from Fredris: "Mother dying wishes to see you. (come) Fredris." I brought the telegram to Capt. Rowsell, he read it and smiled, "Sorry Morry," he said, "you'd be surprised how many of *our boys' relatives have died since coming here. You'll have to wait till tomorrow." And as I could not get him to believe that I was telling the truth I had to wait. The next day I went again when we got paid so again I got my friend the Sgt. to put me on guard duty and let me off before day. Caught the train again and arrived in Edinburgh really early about 5 a.m.. Rang the bell. Fredris thought 'twas the mail or a telegram as usual. Just opened the door to peep, and put out a hand which I grabbed and hauled her out in the hall in her nightclothes. We had a good laugh. Went to see Mrs. Minty at noon time and she was nearly gone. When they told her I was there she just turned towards me and smiled and held out her hand and pulled me down so she could speak to me. She was dying but she gave me a nice smile, whispered my name, and held her hand out to me.*

TO MY BEST CHUM—MY FATHER.
Dear old Dad, when Kitchener called,
    On me to come up with the Boys;
I thought of you and my dear old home,
    And the scenes of my childhood joys.

It's up to me to go out and help,
    The other brave chaps at the Front,
Never let it be said I was one that jibbed
    While others bore the brunt.

When "Ours" go where this picture tells,
    And I hope that won't be long;
We'll get the Huns well on the run,
    To the tune of our marching song.

Memories of Home and my Dear Ones,
    Are ever with me night and day;
Those happy times I shall never forget,
    While at Acreknowe or over the way.
From Howard. Marsh Acreknowe Camp
                                    1915

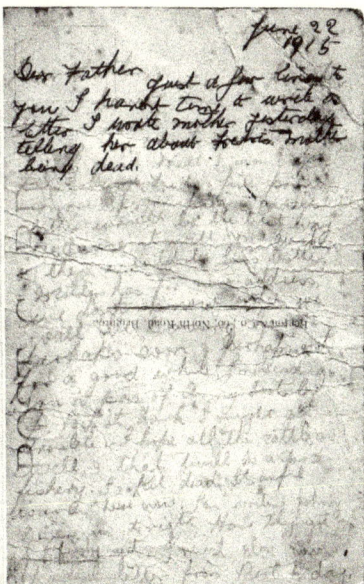

Postcard from Howard Leopold Morry to his father, dated June 22, 1915, informing him of the death of Howard's mother-in-law, Mary Minty, and asking that 5 pounds extra be expedited to Fredris to help out. But also note he mentions sending his father a pair of army boots by freight and to "keep it dark," meaning not to say anything to anyone or he would be in big trouble.

She could just whisper and said, "Be good to my little bairn" and then I said, "When I see you on the other side, I'll be able to look you right straight in the face." She smiled and turned in to the wall and was dead in a minute. Just seemed as if she stayed alive long enough to get my promise which I surely kept to the best of my ability. A jolly woman, and she must have been missed an awful lot after that.

I tried to get to Edinburgh for her funeral and again they thought I was swinging the lead, so I had to wait till next pay day and then to my surprise Capt. Bernard passed me ten days pay besides my regular pay and said that they had reconsidered my case and owing to my previous good record had decided to remit my fine. I thanked him very much and I still think that it was wholly through Capt. Bernard's good offices that it was remitted.

I again got a weekend pass for Edinburgh and arrived there at 5 a.m.. Found them all in bed but got in after a while. I had got one of our Sergeants to put me on guard duty and, as we always got a day off after being on guard duty, this made three days for me. Fredris was looking sick, being fretting very much over her mother's death. She came to meet me at the Waverly Station but my train was in long before she expected it and so I was home before her. These were happy weekends; we enjoyed them to the full, never giving much thought to what the future might have in store for us. We spent our weekend around sight-seeing, taking in the shows and visiting Fredris' friends etc. Got back to camp again on Monday morning in time for parade and so escaped for not having been there at call at lights out.

We were expecting to leave now at any day and so the week passed swiftly. This time again, I was up against it when I looked for a weekend pass. I had had almost every weekend and still, when refused by the Sergeant who I went to for a pass in the absence of our Captain, I did not take no for an answer. I just beat it again, and stayed for the usual three days. The thought of future punishment was the least of my worries.

When I got back to camp, I again stole in and got a good night's sleep. I had stayed three days this time. Alas again arrested on parade for being AWOL, put in the guard tent. The Old Limey Sgt. was marching me off to be tried by the Colonel. Our Captain saw me and said "Sgt. that man is not for headquarters orderly room. I'll try him." I was put at the end of the line of defaulters to be tried by him. When my turn came he again read the charge against me and then asked why I broke leave again. I said "I asked the Sergeant Major Sir, but he wouldn't give me a pass." He said "why did you not come to me." I said "you were away Sir." So he gave me 3 days C.B. which means "confined to barracks." And that was fine of him. He was a good trump, a French Canadian by birth, and taught school in Bishop Feild College in St. John's. He was a great man to handle men. He was well liked by us all. A real man's man. He married Governor Harris' daughter, and she told her waiting maid Armorel, who married a chum of mine, Harold Andrews, that he, Bernard, had naughty little ways, and knowing him as we did, I guess he had. Well he is dead many a year now and I hope that God will be as mild with him, in any of his little escapades as he was with us.

Harold Andrews (left) and Howard Morry before departing Britain.

To hear Howard Morry tell it, the time the Newfoundlanders spent at Stobs Camp was an endless battle of wits between the

officers and the enlisted men intent on sneaking away on unautho-
rised leave. While that was no doubt the case, and would have been
true of other men with less reason to break the rules than Howard,
who did so to marry his sweetheart and say goodbye to his mother-in-law on her deathbed, a great deal of serious training did take
place. Training that would come into play sooner than some of the
more recent recruits, like Howard, might have imagined.

The details of the training they underwent can only be found in
secondary sources; the official war diary of the Royal Newfoundland
Regiment begins on September 1, 1915, the day the Regiment
embarked from Alexandria for the Peninsula. Col. Gerald W. L.
Nicholson, author of *The Fighting Newfoundlander*, was perhaps
the first researcher to delve into the details of the training that the
men underwent in the various phases of their preparation for war.
He describes their training in this manner:

> The Regiment lost no time in getting down seriously to the
> business at hand. The training day began early and ended late.
> Reveille was at 5:30 a.m., and the last parade of the day usually
> did not finish before 4:45 p.m. And if a company had to go

Howard Morry (second from left) and mates just before departing Britain.

to the ranges for its musketry practice—generally a ten day stint—the long work day stretched from half-past four in the morning to eight o'clock at night...The monotony of squad and company drill became less tedious when balanced with such strenuous activities as bayonet fighting. How vigorously they leaped across trenches to charge those straw-filled sacks, 'killing' them with vicious lunge, parry and thrust! The issue of trenching tools led to prodigious exertions at digging trenches, and such words as parapet, travers and parados were added to the vocabulary. Even the twenty-one mile route marches over dusty roads with the burden of a fifty-pound pack brought relatively few complaints.

Even with this rigorous training regime, Newfoundlanders being Newfoundlanders, Nicholson went on to describe how they put to practical use their new rifles, with rabbit stew supplementing the soldiers' limited diet in many of the men's tents.

By now, in July of 1915, the inexperienced baymen and the soft townies of Newfoundland were becoming tough, battle-ready troops. They believed they were ready for action, and most were impatient to get on with it and give the Kaiser something to think about. So when the day finally came to entrain to the south, the rumour was they were headed for France and Belgium and would soon be in the thick of it. As we will learn, that was not to be the case, at least not immediately. For, after a brief period of final and most likely superfluous training on the Salisbury Plain, the Royal Newfoundland Regiment did indeed embark, but not for Europe. The brass had another objective in mind—one that would require seasoning to hot weather, not the cold and the damp of the trenches in Europe.

The RNR and ANZACs in Egypt

The Royal Newfoundland Regiment and the ANZACs were both involved in the Peninsula campaign (perhaps better known as the Dardanelles campaign), as were Ghurkhas and others from widely dispersed parts of the British Commonwealth, but no forces from Canada were deployed to Gallipoli. While, understandably, many published Canadian accounts of WWI written in the past have bypassed this important theatre of war, the moment Newfoundland joined Confederation in 1949, Canadian history absorbed the sacrifices made at Gallipoli. It is therefore rather disappointing to Newfoundlanders that so little attention has been directed toward this unique and important event in Canadian history.

Most of those sent, with the exception of recruits and some regular members of the British Army who had not previously served in India or South Africa, were accustomed to the heat and other environmental conditions that were anticipated in Turkey. Certainly most of the Australians and New Zealanders were familiar with the hot temperatures. But this could not be said for the Newfoundlanders. One wonders if the decision to send Newfoundlanders had to do with the knowledge, not widely shared by the common soldier at the outset, that although the summer in that area was abysmally hot, the winter was quite the opposite. The tables were essentially turned, with the Newfoundlanders—who were accustomed to ice, sleet, and extreme cold—being more able to cope with the harsh winter conditions in Gallipoli than the warm-blooded ANZACs and others. To some extent, it must have been expected that the troops accustomed to one set of environmental conditions would help the others by providing clues on how to cope.

The Royal Newfoundland Regiment only arrived in Suvla Bay on September 19, 1915. The ANZACs and other British Forces had already been locked in a stalemate with the Turks for nearly five months since their initial arrival at Cape Helles and ANZAC Cove on April 25 of that year. Despite these reinforcements, no real progress was made in driving back the Turks, and it was finally decided by high command to abandon this failed strategy in December of 1915, with the first withdrawals at Suvla Bay and surrounding areas on the 19th, and the final withdrawal at Cape Helles on January 8-9, 1916. In all, the campaign is estimated to have caused upwards of 265,000 casualties amongst the British and their allies, with as many as 46,000 killed in action or due to exposure and disease, as well as perhaps 218,000 casualties and 66,000 deaths on the Turkish side. These numbers remain unverified due to confusion in the campaign. ANZAC casualties are better quantified: the Australians alone suffered 26,094 casualties with 7594 killed while the New Zealanders suffered 7,571 casualties and 2,431 killed. The RNR lost 44 men, that is certain, and suffered an additional 500 casualties, approximately, among the 1076 who landed, matching, if not exceeding, the casualty rate of the other larger contingents.

Another aspect of the Peninsula campaign that has not received due attention in the histories written in Canada and elsewhere is that the Newfoundlanders, among others, were chosen to remain behind to the bitter end in the rearguard action during the evacuations, not only at Suvla Bay, but also later at Cape Helles. While the ANZACs' courageous efforts and staggering losses at Gallipoli are remembered in song (e.g., "And the Band Played Waltzing Matilda") and commemorated each year on ANZAC Day (April 25), not so the sacrifices of the RNR which, though smaller in number, were equal in scale according to their impact on the regiment. Howard Morry's narrative does correct these oversights to some extent. This next section begins with the departure of Companies A through D from Stobs Camp on August 2, 1915, en route to Aldershot in the south of England prior to embarking for their real encounter with history in Egypt, the Peninsula, and the European theatre of war.

Well time and tide waits for no man and the day at length came, when we got leave to go and say goodbye to our friends in Edinburgh. Mont and I went down together. I was in Edinburgh in a short time and I can tell you, five days how quickly they pass on a time like that, when you are spending them with someone you love and may never see again. Well, it came time to go. Fredris and I went in her bedroom and knelt by the bedside and said a few short prayers, that I might be spared to come back again. Fredris and her dad and sisters came to the station, where the troop train was and she looked very sad and sick too. A lot of troops, Newfoundlanders, along with some Scottish Soldiers, were bidding their friends, wives and sweethearts farewell. When the goodbyes were said we went through the gates to the train and 'twas all over. I never saw Fredris again for over two years and Phyllis [their first child] was able to run around. I said goodbye and sat by the window and waved to Fredris and her father as we pulled out of the Station and then we realised our fun was pretty well over, and the other part of the business had to start.

Mont and I got in to camp late as usual that night. It was raining hard and we did not have any money for a bus, so we had to hike the five miles from the station to camp. Then we had to go through a large field of turnips to make a detour to get past the guards, which we did safely. And, speaking of turnips, the farmers around there presented a pretty large bill to our C.O.

for damages to their turnip crops. We must have ate about two hundred barrels of turnips while we were there. They could not understand people eating raw turnips. But after all, our fellows would sooner have a good turnip than a good apple. To get on with my story, it poured rain all night and when I got in our bell tent, I snuggled down in the warmest place I could get. And, as there were 13 in each bell tent, it was quite a squeeze, as we all slept around in a circle with our feet towards the pole. However after a while I sank down between two of the boys, and slept the sleep of the Just. I'd like to be able to sleep now, like I could then. We struck camp about 2 p.m. that afternoon and boarded a train for an unknown destination. We were packed as tight as we could stow and put in a hard night, but in the morning we detrained and marched to Barracks in Aldershot, where we had to stay for a while to get a thorough training before going overseas.

We were put through a rigorous training for about three weeks [only sixteen days actually]. *We did not get any time for any amusement of any kind. At last the order came to leave. So at night we boarded a train bound for we knew not where and in all the Annals of the British Army I don't think there was a more disorderly mob left the "Hub of Discipline," Aldershot, where, if you had one button open, you'd be sent back to barracks for carelessness and being improperly dressed. Instead of marching, we walked, and those of us that were sober had the worst of it, for we had to look out for the other fellows. We were in full marching order, and besides had our kit bags, and it is beyond comprehension how we got to the train and got all aboard between fighting and coaxing. I knew the Officers of the Regular Army were mad enough to cry. But we being Colonials and volunteers, they were forced to shut their eyes to our shortcomings. But our Colonel knew his men though, for he said when these fellows get down to business there will be no stopping them, and he was right.*

Well, sometime next morning we arrived at Portsmouth [in fact they arrived in Devonport, a part of Plymouth, not

Newfoundland Regiment Drum and Bugle Band, Aldershot, England, 1915.

Portsmouth, on August 20, 1915, and departed that same day], *and about 7 a.m. began marching on board ship, four deep. One old lady who lived near was by the gate crying as we were marching through and she said "every day for a year I've seen men marching down this wharf and how few come back." And it was nearly noon before we were all aboard. The Majestic I think was her name. We could not see it as anything the name was on was removed or covered up for security reasons.* [The name was *Megantic*—named after Lake Megantic in Quebec—and she was part of the White Star line, operating on the Canada route until requisitioned as a troopship during wwI.]

We soon pulled out and that was our last sight of Portsmouth for many a day. That evening at sunset leaning over the rail I could see the White Cliffs of Dover receding from view. How many there were of us who never saw them again. Some we left in Suez, some in Cairo, some in the Peninsula in lonely graves, far away from their homeland.

There was a battalion of English troops on her as well as us, the Warwicks, going down for a garrison duty at Khartoum. They were all middle-aged men, most of them having served 21 years in the Army. We all slept on deck going down the

Mediterranean and when the crew began washing the decks in the morning we had to wake up and get out of the way. But we sure got a good sleep, not like the guys who slept below. The heat down there was stifling.

The Destroyer steamed round and round us till we were well away from Britain's shore, and then we carried on our way till we reached the Straits of Gibraltar and were again convoyed safely to Malta [August 26, 1915]. We were there a couple of days while they were rounding up some German U-Boats and some of the boys got passes on shore, but I did not.

We went into Malta, but only a few were allowed on shore. The rest of us just stayed on board and looked and wished. There were 7 Battalions of troops on that ship and she was packed pretty well I can tell you.

The *Megantic* was a cruise ship, both before and after the war, having survived at least one U-Boat attack, and was refitted for first-class service after the war. No doubt the Newfoundland troops that sailed on her to Egypt in heat and discomfort would find it rather ironic that posh services for the wealthy would be the norm on board a few years later.

It is one of those strange coincidences in life that, just as Howard Morry was embarking on the *Megantic* for the Mediterranean on August 20, 1915, his wife, already pregnant with their first child, was halfway across the Atlantic on the Athenia, en route to her new

The ss Megantic *as it appeared when in use as a troop carrier.*

home in Ferryland via Quebec City. So they were both sailing at the same time, heading in opposite directions: Fredris to safety and Howard into battle.

Fredris never returned to Scotland. One can only imagine the shock that greeted this educated, well-bred Edinburgh lassie upon her arrival in Ferryland, where there was no electricity, telephone service, radio reception, nor roads worthy of the name.

We left Malta after staying there a few days and started off for the Dardanelles. We passed through numerous dead bodies of men and horses from a transport ship that preceded us and had been torpedoed. It made us feel more determined.

After leaving Malta, we got an epidemic of diarrhea or dysentery or something on board and hundreds of the men went down with it. You can imagine the mess, the latrines were crowded all the time, and everywhere you looked men had their pants down. The hoses were kept slushing down the decks all the time. I got it pretty bad. I never experienced such pain. I lay on the hatch and rolled and moaned for hours. Then a couple of my friends, Frank Le Messurier, and Bill Viguers, found me and got Capt. Donnelly. He gave me a tumbler full of brandy, while they were looking for the doctor. It did not seem to do me a bit of good. Sometimes through the night I'd fall asleep. But I was sure busy three or four days, and felt quite weak when we landed. The Warwicks, who are older men, suffered a lot, and lost quite a few men. We blamed the food. We had bologna about three times a day and got fed up on it. We made several complaints to our officers, and at last after having shoved a lot of tables with food and everything on them overboard, got our case brought before the C.O. He said he could not do anything about it, but our Colonel Burton told him that he'd better do something as our boys were desperate and could take the ship and sail her to any part of the world, as we could, as there were navigators, engineers and sailors galore in our lot. Anyway we got a change in diet and got rid of the dysentery.

In the next section of his diary, Howard neglects to mention that they briefly made port at the Greek Island of Mudros before turning back to Egypt. What he and the other men did not know at the time was that they turned back because a part of the British contingent on board was urgently called to support the garrison in the Sudan. The official war diary of the Royal Newfoundland Regiment begins only on September 1, 1915, with the arrival in Alexandria of the *Megantic*. Events that transpired prior to that time, both in Britain and the Mediterranean, must be deduced from consulting other mainly unofficial accounts.

For some reason we turned back from the Peninsula and the next place we found ourselves was in Cairo [the Port of Alexandria actually]. *My mother's sister Matilda* [Mathilda White], *who had married Capt. Richard Prior, was living there. He was Captain on one of the P&O Liners. Mont and I went to the Colonel to get leave to go on shore. He asked us why we wished to go on shore, and I told him I had an aunt living there. He smiled and said it's astonishing how many Newfoundland women are living here. So he refused us a pass. I thought of Capt. Carthy who was a friend of the family and he got us a pass on shore.*

We were delighted and landed in that town of smells and disease of all kinds. It was a great adventure to us, our first time on shore in a foreign port, an Eastern one at that. Everything interested us; the Egyptians with all their funny ways, the veiled women, especially; you'd see their eyes gleaming through the slits in their head covering, I just forget the name now; the merchants with their wares out on the sidewalks; the beggars holding out their hands for buckshee; and the camels and donkeys in galore. The voices and noises of all made it seem strange and unreal to us. Very few whites, to be seen and those were mostly French and Greek and Italian and spoke broken English. We wandered up and down the streets looking for my aunt's address. At length an English officer told us where to go for

*the European residential quarter and we got there in the early
afternoon. Had to go up three flights of stairs on the outside of
the houses.*

*At last we came to the address and just then, a little bit away
in a roof garden we saw two white girls sitting in the shade of
some ornamental trees. They bowed and gave us a nice smile,
which we returned, and we passed a few words with them and
I found out that the light haired girl was my cousin Mary, who
had married a man called Quintana who, at that time, was
head Censor for the Government.*

The grandson of Mary, John Quinn, provided information on
this marriage in 2001, noting that Mary Prior married William
Quintana, and they lived in Alexandria, Egypt. In 1939 the name
was changed by deed poll from Quintana to Quinn. They had five
children all now deceased: John's father, Gerald, John, Vernon
(killed in the war), May and Yoland. His great grandfather, John
Quintana, lived on the island of Syra, Greece, where he was the
British vice consul. He was married to Eugenie Rosier, and they had
fourteen children all born on the island.

*Just then the sliding wicket on the door slid back and a dark
face looked at us through the iron bars and asked us our business, and I told him we were two soldiers from Newfoundland
that wanted to see Mrs. Prior. At that moment my aunt came
along and unbarred the door and let us in. What a welcome
we got. She hadn't seen a person from here for over thirty
years and she kept piling questions on us for hours. We had a
great time, till about nine o'clock p.m. when we were ushered
into a large room with about fifty guests, the gentlemen all
in evening dress and the ladies. Well! It was a great experience for us, two outharbour boys, who never knew very much
about style, but who were quite polite in our own way. After
introductions were over, we sat down to dine. It seems my
cousin's husband had given a banquet to a lot of big shots that*

evening and it spoke well for him to have us there, and not poke us away in a side room or someplace, which we would have preferred.

Well as I said, we sat down, Mont and I, side by side, with a nice old lady on each side of us to keep us company. I was so shy that the perspiration was pouring off me, and Mont was just as bad. It did not take us long to see that there was a bottle of the best whisky at each of our right hands, as there was to every person male and female at the table, and the attendants were sure to keep your tumbler filled. After a few shots we felt quite calm and collected and began to enjoy ourselves. And by the time it came around to the liqueurs, Absinthe, etc., we were pretty well back to normal, and when the others drank we did likewise. When it was all over we told some stories and answered a lot of questions and before we knew it our time was up and we had to get back to the ship. So my cousin drove us in his car to the ship. We had a very enjoyable evening, and though I never saw my cousins or aunt again, they wrote us often when we were in the Peninsula and sent us many cigarettes and other comforts. When we were leaving in the morning, they gave us 1,000 cigarettes, which were very welcome to all the boys, as we gave them away right and left, as neither of us smoked very much.

When we arrived at the wharf where the steamer was, we met our chaps marching ashore, so we just had time to grab our packs and rifles and join them. We boarded a train and were whisked off in the night. And next morning we saw the sun rising like a ball of fire out of the desert. It was an awful hot uncomfortable drive, packed like sardines in third class railway carriages. The heat was intense, and the only place we could get a breath was out between the cars on the platform and steps. I sat on a step for hours and only got up out of it when I found myself dropping off asleep. I was afraid I'd fall off and be killed.

We had great fun with the Egyptians, who came to the stations with fruit. At first we would get to buy it, but as time went on and money got scarce, some of our chaps enticed the

Egyptians quite near and then surrounded them and took all the fruit they had. It was laughable to see an Egyptian tearing away over the desert, with a basket or tray of fruit on his head, and the rags streaming around him, and a bunch of our boys trying to cut them off. This kind of thing went on for a few stations, but eventually the officers found it out and put an end to it.

That train ride seems like a bad dream to me, I don't know how long we were on her. I don't remember how many days or hours or anything, all I remember is heat, sand and flies, and hunger and thirst. At length the train pulled in to a station and we detrained and were marched through the streets to our barracks. After we found that it was Abbasieh [Abbassia] Barracks at Cairo. We were formed up on the parade ground and after being given our places in barracks, we were dismissed for breakfast.

Me and my chums, seeing the gate open and no one on guard, wandered out through it and across the street to a restaurant, where we got a meal and a few bottles of Egyptian Beer, which I believe is the worst drink on earth (camel's piss the Aussies called it, and I don't think they were far out, awful stuff). After eating we went to the town and everywhere we looked, we saw our boys and Australian troops intermingled. So we went with the rest and soon had some pals of our own among the Australians and, being of the same blood and wild nature as themselves, they soon made us wise to what to do and how to get around in Egypt.

We were such apt pupils, that on that very afternoon I was on a streetcar and when the conductor came to take our money or tickets some of our boys at once threw him off, and when the driver stopped the car to take him on, he was immediately packed off and an Australian and one of our boys took charge. We went all over Cairo and some of us got off at Shepheard Hotel [famous colonial-era hotel in Cairo], where anyone that knows anything about Cairo goes. Among the bunch were Willis White, Harry Mifflin, Lewis Head, Davey Carew, Watty

Thomas, and a lot more I forget. Anyway, in we went and had a few drinks of real beer before some R P's [Regimental Police] came to arrest us. But they did not interfere with the Aussies. They did not stand for any different treatment between officers and privates. But at that time over 40 years ago it was sure carried out in the British Army. Privates could not be seen walking even with Non-coms who were friends and neighbours back home. We did not bother about keeping away from our Non-coms. We had some wonderful sergeants, among them Joe McKinley, Charlie Watson, Ed Higgins, in fact they were all pretty good. After an hour or so, the thought of returning to barracks never entered our minds. We drank beer and whisky and sang and danced till we were tired. Gradually, our fellows began to get scarce. Me and my chums, Harold Andrews and Harry Mifflin, decided to go back to barracks, where we were joined by Fred Janes and Dan Costello. When we got there we saw Capt. Donnelly with seven "C" Company fellows on parade, and he reading the Kings Regs. to them. We just took a pop through the gate and beat it again.

This time we got in a street car again. We were just on when an Aussie came along and asked us where we wanted to go, and we said the big pyramid. He said "OK I'll stand the gaff," so we thanked him very much and we did not see him again until he had driven the streetcar as far as the track went, and then some in the sand. He showed us where the pyramids were and got a guide for us and then bade us goodbye saying, "I've got a date at the other end of the dump," meaning Cairo, and that he did not want to be picked up by the police. He gave as his name "Burroughs" and wished us luck and told us to always keep in with the boys from down under and we would be O.K. And we did, they were a great bunch, and called us the Little Newfoundlanders.

We went out to the Pyramids and what a sight for us. Had to get a guide to look after our boots and puttees, which we took off in order to crawl up through the interior of the Great

Pyramid, to the burial vault at the top. It was about 20 ft. long and almost eight foot wide. The roof was composed of six slabs of polished stone, fitted so close together that you could scarcely see the seams between them. The stone steps leading up to the chamber were worn down in the middle till there was no sign of a step. You put your hands on the sides, or rather ends of the steps that were not worn out and dragged ourselves up. How many millions of pilgrims did it take to wear these stone steps like that in the course of six thousand years?

Harold Mifflin and Harold Andrews, two of Howard Morry's chums.

Well to get on with my story, when we came down again, we found we had some trouble on our hands, as our boots and puttees had been taken from the fellow we gave them to, to mind for us, and a different Egyptian had each boot and puttee and wanted buckshee money before they gave them back. However, after about a half hour of promises and threats, a few well-placed kicks with our army boots, or rather the boot of these chaps who had just come along to go up, we got ours and held theirs for them till they came down, and this is the procedure we followed for the rest of our stay in Egypt. And the guides, instead of having easy marks to deal with, got the wrong end of the stick.

After spending a while there we had a look at the Sphinx, went under it and around it and, at last just before sundown, wearily wended our way back to Cairo. When we arrived at the end of the car line we found a car just waiting, which we boarded and put our fare this time, got off at Abbassia Barracks, and reported to Headquarters and got a talking to about a soldier's duty etc. but were let off very lightly. Spent that night and slept on the stone floors it was cold as could be. We had only just found out how cold the nights in Egypt could be.

Next day, we fell in as usual, done some drill and got dismissed after about an hour. Everyone got leave, only not those who were on duty. Found the day very hot. I spent the great part of it laying down with my mouth to the grating of a cellar or basement in one of the hallways of the barracks. There was a grand cool breeze coming through and it wasn't long till I had chums, all laying around for a turn at the grating and smoking, singing etc. to pass the time.

At night we went to the famous Wazit [Wazzir] red light district. Mont Windsor, his brother Stan, and I went together and what a sight! Hundreds of soldiers of all countries going in and out of the houses, the girls were reaping their harvest, and some of the soldiers, the Aussies especially, got something that made the rest of their lives a living hell. Some of the houses were five and six stories high with balconies and curtained windows where the girls sat around in various attitudes and with very little on them. Some had thin veils, others had less than that, and they did everything to appeal to the primitive passions of man. Still I must say the vast majority, especially our fellows, kept away. But these houses were sure busy with the Aussies and some of our boys as well. We were standing on a corner, watching and talking to a couple of Aussies when a Padre came along and said "boys, think of your mothers and wives and sisters at home." One of them took out his pocketbook and said, "I'll stand you a go Parson." We felt awful ashamed. The poor Padre walked away.

Shortly after we arrived there we heard screams and yells from a block of houses across the street and next we saw the girls all streaming out of them, while from overhead pianos and all kinds of things came hurtling down in the street, and next a great blaze burst out. The Aussies had set fire to it. Some of their pals had got diseases there that could not be cured, so these guys took the law in their own hands and burnt the whole thing down. They said at that time Cairo was the worst city in

Cousins in uniform. Four cousins of Howard Morry who survived the war: CQMS. Wilfred Montgomery Windsor (top left), L. Cpl. Stanley Charles Windsor (top right), Pte. Francis Ernest Le Messurier (at Stobs Camp), and Lieut. Philip Sorsoleil Le Messurier (bottom right). The latter was in for the entire duration and rose from ordinary foot soldier through the ranks to Lieutenant.

the world—there were thirty thousand licensed scarlet women there—and, from what I saw, I quite believe it.

About half an hour after the fire started I was taken with severe cramps in the stomach and Mont and I left to try to get back to Barracks. The pain was frightful and I used to double up and lie down on the street. Mont went looking for a Red Cross man or an ambulance. I don't know how long he was gone, as I was wandering along in a semi-conscious condition. By and by, I remember Mont came along with a bunch of Australians in a touring car, and they took me in and gave me a drink of some kind that made me feel better, and after a little while I began to sweat and shiver. However I took a few more drinks and took some interest in my companions. They were a gay crowd and we spent a few hours doing the town and, all of a sudden I got another attack, and after that I don't remember. Mont told me they took me to our hospital camp and there I was bad for a good many days and lost a lot of fun.

However I got out again about the time we moved out of Barracks to camps out in the desert, about four miles outside of Cairo [Polygon Camp]. *The camps were big marquees that would hold about fifty men easy, but there were only about fifteen of us in each camp and we had lots of room. They were doubled, the inside camp was heavily padded with cotton to the depth of 4 or 5 inches, just like a quilt, and outside that with about a foot of air space was the ordinary canvas camp. Still when the sun got up a bit, we lay panting and sweating, with our mouths down to the edge of the inside camp trying to get a breath of fresh air and that is the way we passed our days, it was too hot to drill, except an hour before day and the same in the evening.*

Just as the sun was sinking in the west each evening we could see the Egyptians coming in from Cairo, with their donkeys for hire, and it was a sight. With their long white clothes fluttering in the wind, as they drove their donkeys and ran beside them, to try to be first to get a fare. Then the rush began and such a noise, each one yelling of the virtues of their donkeys, and our fellows trying to cut down the prices. At last we would all leave for town, and that indeed was a sight. Some big fellows like myself on a little donkey whose back was hollowed right down, and we could stick our toes in the sand as we passed along. The small fellows had the best of it. They got to town quicker, and very often out-raced the owner of the donkey, and when they arrived in the city, just gave the donk a slap on the rump and made off without bothering to pay or anything else.

I haven't any idea how long we were there, but at last one fine morning we boarded the train and we were off [September 14, 1915]. *The usual bunch of Egyptians at the railway stations and along the embankments or cuts shouting or shaking their baubles at us as we passed. They always reminded me of monkeys in the zoo. After staying on the train for hours we were worn out with the heat and smells. Now and then we would go out and sit on the steps between the cars and get a breath of cool air. As before, I was afraid to sit two long, as one was, lest we would doze asleep and fall off. In fact one of our boys, young Hannaford, did fall off and, what was almost a miracle, escaped without a scratch.*

The dysentery was still bothering me a lot and at the end of our journey I was again placed in a field hospital where I stayed till the morning we were leaving for the Dardanelles. The doctor came in and said to the seven of us who were in the tent "who's for the front" and we all stood up except one. I often thought afterward, what fools we were to leave for the front before we were cured, or what was the matter with our doctor to pass us fit. I was the only one of that bunch who came back from the Dardanelles; the rest of them all died up there. And only for I was exceptionally strong and tough, the cold weather came in time I guess, I would have too. My weight went down from 208 lbs. when I left England to 126; just a skeleton. I suffered there from the day we landed till we left it, and on times to this very day.

The Dardanelles Campaign
and Gallipoli

The events that follow have all but been forgotten by Canadian historians outside of Newfoundland. Many of the official preparations for the commemorating of the events of Canada at war in WWI have skipped over or failed to even recognize the fact that Canadians, albeit Newfoundlanders at the time, were engaged in this fateful and, as history records, futile venture. British-led forces, mostly ANZACs but also Newfoundlanders and others, were deployed to wrest control of the Gallipoli Peninsula and the all-important channel known as the Dardanelles, connecting the Mediterranean to the Black Sea, from the Turks. Had they been successful, this would have freed the allied Russian fleet to escape the confines of its bases in Crimea and join the fray in the Mediterranean and the Atlantic. A combination of poor planning and bad decision making by general staff, a superior Turkish force, impossible terrain, disastrous climatic conditions, and rampant diseases in the trenches all contributed to this monumental failure.

Howard Morry wrote his remembrances of these events in his memoirs for the first time on January 15, 1943. Another great war was raging at that time, and two of his sons were involved in the fight, one on land with the British Army (Bill) and the other at sea with the Royal Navy (Reg). Given that twenty-eight years had passed since he lived through these awful experiences, it is a testament to how memorable the events were that he remembered them in such fine detail. He later re-wrote his memoires in 1957 and again in the 1960s, but it is likely he fell back upon this version to refresh his memory at those later times.

Jan 15, 1943

It's over two years since I wrote any. I've been so busy with the present. I had not time to think or write of the past. I find it very hard to do the work around. I wish the war was over and the boys home. Several more of my chums of 14 and 18 have crossed the divide. Frank Dooley, Shandy Benson, Ralph Cooper, and others I just can't call to mind. I got letters all along from my real buddy, Harold Andrews, who now lives in England. And one night last spring a knock came at our door and a voice said "is there an old "C" Company fellow living here?" I said "yes come in!" It was Roy Spencer, an old chum and a good trump. He had a couple of friends with him. They were going salmon fishing. But as the bottle passed around, and we got yarning, fishing became a secondary affair, and his visit of a few minutes stretched into hours. We yarned and sang all the old songs and told some experiences. It was great to see him again and, though he was minus an arm and half a foot, he was as lively as ever.

Once again, Howard neglects to mention much in the way of details on this passage, including the name of the vessel, HMT *Ausonia,* or the intermediate port of call on September 18, 1915, at Mudros. While this was only a brief landing for the purpose of getting organised for the landing at Suvla Bay on the HMT *Prince Abbas* the following day, it would seem remarkable enough to be recorded in his memoirs. I suspect his illness was more distracting than his memoirs let on, and that he was oblivious to most of what was happening during these days. The same seems to have been the case in the interval between the aftermath of Beaumont-Hamel and the arrival of the Newfoundland Regiment at Ypres.

On our arrival at the Dardanelles, after escaping submarines etc., we were landed in big barges and were under fire right away. When the first shells pitched near us, we all began scrambling for pieces of them, though quite hot, for souvenirs. We got lots of souvenirs without looking for them before long. We had quite a few wounded that day. It was hot work digging in under fire.

In the afternoon, we were marched up from the beach to a gully or ravine for shelter. Then we were at war, and we began to realise it too. As we were marching along, a shell burst near and a piece of it was rolling along by us, when one of our boys, Mike Walsh of St. John's, put out his foot to stop it and it took the best part of his foot off. The war was over as far as he was concerned.

That night we spent in the rear of the trenches, but we had sentries out and I'll always remember it, as the sound of bullets went whispering by, while from the trenches we could hear the burst of an occasional shell and the steady crack and roar of rifle fire.

We spent three days mixed with the Royal Scots for experience, and then took over our own part of the line. The Scots were a great bunch. We always got on well with them.

On the first night we were in the line I was one of a digging party sent out under Sgt. Harold Mitchell to dig a new firing line or trench. In that patrol were, myself, Jackie Davis, Harold Andrews, Davey Carew and the others I forget. 'Twas a cloudy night, but when the clouds passed the moon shone brightly. While we were waiting to go out, I whispered to Harold this looks like "A Dirty Night on the Crossroads" (one of Capt. Bairnsfather's sketches).

Bairnsfather was a popular cartoonist of the day whose works, published in *The Bystander*, starting in 1915, took on somewhat of a propaganda slant during the war.

We were only seventy yards from the Turks. We were extended six paces from each other and them started digging. We were not five minutes at it when the Turks opened fire on us and hit two Scotsmen. I heard one say "Oh my bloody back" when they were bringing him in. There were seven of us and six Scots. We got an order to lie down, which we did, and we hugged the ground too, I can tell you. After a few minutes we got the order to dig again. And that's how it was all night.

In the morning, we were down about four feet by daylight and then our day party was sent in and we were relieved. The new party had not been in an hour when one of my little buddies, Davey Carew, was killed by a sniper [October 7, 1915]. *He forgot, and stood up to straighten his back and lost his life doing so. He was just about eighteen, and only two nights before he asked if he could share his blanket with me, as he felt lonely. I suppose, me being older than him, he thought he was OK when he was with me. When he was detailed for duty that morning, I was just going to lie down on the firestep, where we always lay together. He said "I'm finished now, they are taking me away from you." I laughed at him, but he looked awful sad. Four or five of the younger kids always hung around me. I was ten to twelve years older than them and they seemed to think I'd keep them safe. They were Dave Carew, Billy Short, Chan Freebairn & Harold Andrews. The latter became a real good pal of mine through the years. Chan died of some kind of fever on the Peninsula. Just lived one day after being taken out of the trenches* [records indicate October 23, 1915. He is buried at Addolorata Cemetery, Malta]. *I missed Davey a lot. Next day his two brothers and I buried him under a big oak tree. God rest you Davey. I often think of you, and can see your lonely grave* [Hill 10 Cemetery, Gallipoli].

The official regimental war diary was extremely terse in reporting casualties such as these. For Davey Carew, the report read, "Fire Trenches—7/10/15—Killed—One." On the other hand, at least such a death merited mention. Those invalided out and succumbing to their wounds or illnesses elsewhere, like Chan Freebairn, received not a mention.

Chan Freebairn and Soper, two of my chums, were very sick one night. I was sent out to the hospital on the beach with Chan. We walked out. I delivered him at the hospital. It took two hours to go two miles, and the last of it I had to carry him. He died next day [records indicate October 23, 1915].

Well we had our share of night patrols, listening patrols etc. And once the Turks got between us and our own lines. We were out without rifles that night, as the previous night one of our boys shot and killed an English officer who did not answer when challenged. He lived long enough to exonerate the chap from all blame, but as a result we were sent out next night with only bayonets for protection and it was a wonder we were not wiped out. We had just one killed and three wounded out of our patrol. Lieut. Cyril Carter, the officer in charge, was badly wounded; he would not let us bring him in till all his men were accounted for. A chap, Brown (I don't know what his first name was, "Gravy" we used to call him, he belonged Placentia way), was shot in the leg, and I saw Mike Downey pick him up and throw him over his shoulder to bring him in when, suddenly, I saw a Turk taking aim at him with his rifle. I saw the flash and heard Brown groan again. Mike Downey was one of the biggest and strongest men I ever saw, a quiet, nice chap. The officers had quite a time with him trying to get him to salute them, and stand at attention while talking to them. It was a scramble for us to get in through the Turks but we managed it pretty good; we dodged and ran till we made it. After that, we went armed when we went on patrol.

It is a curious anomaly that, while Newfoundlanders are always interested in a new acquaintance's genealogy (often asking, "Now who might you be?" or "Who do you belong to?"), many have seemed oblivious to just how interrelated we truly are. In a small, isolated population like that of Newfoundland, how could it be otherwise? From the above account it is obvious that Howard had no idea he was related to Lieut. Cyril Carter. They were both descended from the same immigrant stock—Robert and Ann Carter—who defended Ferryland from French attack in the late 1700s. Albeit, that relationship was rooted in the distant past.

Things went on day by day much the same. Patrols, firing from the trenches; you'd fire at a flash from the Turkish trenches, then walk four or five steps, as right away you'd hear the crack of their firing back at you.

We were beginning to think we were quite forgotten, more than half down with dysentery and fever, no relief, no reinforcements coming. No matter how sick you were, medicine and duty was all you got. Shortly after we dug the new firing line, Capt. Donnelly and a patrol went out and captured a little hill between the lines. We called it Caribou Hill. I remember only two of the men who were with him. Joachim Murphy was killed, and Bill Snow. There was so much firing out there all night that we never expected to see them alive, but they held the hill and only lost a couple of men and three or four wounded.

The days were very hot and the nights cold. Water was very scarce and some days we only had a pint a day for cooking purposes and all. The flies were so thick that you could not see three feet ahead of you in the trench, and it was impossible to keep them wiped out of the corners of your mouth, your nostrils or eyes. You could not keep them away at all. When you opened a can of beef, 'twas black with them before you could get it to your mouth. No wonder we had dysentery. Some got sore eyes and had to be sent back. Then the lice got so thick that we'd get leave for an hour or so each day to go in the back trench and strip and clean our shirts and trousers. Anyone that had a hairy body (I was one of these unfortunates) would spend most of their time scratching. When you'd loosen your puttees to take them off, your legs would be covered as thick as they could stow. We were issued with knitted body belts to keep off cholera. We had to discard them or be eat off in the middle. When the sun would get up a bit, everyone with the exception of the man on the periscope would strip, and anyone who had a bit of a candle was lucky. Turn your pants inside out, turn back the seam, and run a lighted candle or match up and down the seam a few times. Then give them a good beating and put them on again. It didn't seem to matter. After 10 or 12 hours you were as lousy as ever again. The eggs would be maybe a dozen on every hair. It wasn't the fighting we minded, 'twas the heat and flies and lice.

After six weeks there we got our ration of butter; 2 oz. per man per week; figure that out. Very seldom got any cigarettes and there was no place to buy them. When the weather got a bit cooler, I was back in the trenches again after two weeks at the beach. We were glad when we were detailed to go out to the beach after dark for seawater for the officers and men to wash in. We brought it in four gallon oil tins. We also brought the mail when it came. And one lucky night there was about twenty of us sent out for the mail. We had to make two trips. There were about forty bags. We got caught by shellfire on the crossroads; we dropped them and ran for shelter. Jim Gladney (Mount Cashel) was one of the first back. The boys were scattered a bit and he whispered to me "do you smell anything?" I said "yes, whiskey." We found the bag. 'Twas in a mess. It opened our eyes. We now knew why the officers were standing up so well. Just a few we could trust. Took notice of the markings on that particular bag. We got another one and hid it unknown to the rest of the crowd. Just let six fellows in on it. The next night we were not detailed. But the next again we were. And you can imagine our feelings when we stole away down in a ravine and *opened the bag. Four bottles of whisky, cans of ham, potted meats, chicken, Huntley and Palmers Biscuits. What a feed and what a drink! We decided to let the rest of the fellows in on it, and when we got the right sergeant and corporal in charge of us. We were sure to be shelled on the crossroads. I often think that those mail bags saved a lot of our lives.*

We did not get any parcels from home until we got down to Port Tawfik after we evacuated the peninsula, but more about that later. One night going in with the mail and rations daylight caught us before we reached our lines and we lost five or six men. The Turks caught us in the open. That is where Fitzgerald, the Red Cross man, was killed out trying to haul the wounded to shelter and bandage them. His deed is told in the song "The Valley of Kilbride." A real nice chap. His death and the other deaths put a kind of crimp in our adventures with the mail bags for a while.

One night we were waiting at the crossroad for the shelling and machine gun fire to cease when one of the chaps, Lewis Head from Comfort Cove, a real nice chap meant for the ministry—did not drink, smoke, cuss or tell yarns like the most of the rest of us did and always knelt and said his prayers—he was wondering if we'd have to pay for stealing the mailbags in the hereafter. He never had any part of it but could not tell on the rest of us. Anyway we kicked it around for a while and decided that there were a lot of things to be looked at and did not see how God could be hard on anyone who was only trying to live. Dan Moore (Avondale) said God made wine out of water at a wedding and he didn't think there was much difference in that than getting whisky out of mailbags. Dan sure liked his liquor! When we were in training he was always up for being drunk and disorderly. I remember one night after we had been on the peninsula for months we were all sitting on the firestep in our bay, hardly a word then spoken just the crack of bullets overhead. Dan looked up and said "Boys I've just been wondering what a crime sheet looks like." We all had a good laugh. Dan always said he wanted to die with his boots on like a man. He lost a leg in France.

The nights began to get colder and longer and still the days were warm. And the lice and flies just as bad as ever. We just lived from one mail day to another. Mail day was a great event. We opened our mail, swapped the news and talked a lot about home, got the papers and read the war news of course. We did not know anything about the war, only the little piece directly in front of us. We read with much amusement the stories of two of our boys who had arrived home for discharge after only a few days in the trenches.

One of the cruellest things, or the saddest I thought I ever saw, was the look on fellow's faces when the mail came and they did not get any. I could not begin to explain that look. If their relatives at home who did not write could see their faces they would never forget it. Facing death every day and thinking of home and loved ones there who would not even take a few minutes off to write. I often wondered what their thoughts were when they'd see their buddies reading their letters over and over. And for my own self, I'd get a letter from home, read it over and remember every word of it, then burn it and wonder if I'd still be alive when the next letter came.

The nights were long and lonely. One hour on sentry, one lying down on the firestep. Go to sleep with the shells bursting and the noise of rifle fire and wake with them still hard at it. Often, winter nights at home sitting by the fire listening to the cracking of the firewood always reminded me of the intermittent rifle fire on the peninsula. How long the nights were in November and December—got dark before five and was dark for about fourteen hours—and how hungry were we! In fact hunger and food were one of the chief topics of conversation—bully beef, army biscuits and dried vegetables, a handful of prunes now and then, apricot jam once in a while, made chiefly of turnips, two ounces of cheese and two of butter once a week. I often wonder since I came home why we eat so much. I often felt stuffy after a big meal and, thinking back to the army meals, you'd have eaten a quarter as much, always hungry, still strong and fit and able to stand all kinds of hardship.

We were thirty five days in the front line on a stretch in the Dardanelles. General Cayley would come in and ask our officers if we could stick it another few days. He liked us and we him, and our old Colonel Burton, and we him too. We were quite a handful too. Whenever we had a mix-up with the Regulars in our brigade, he always took our part. Once he objected to the High Command that we were getting too much digging to do. He said "those boys came over to fight, not to do all the dirty work." He went off sick, then we had Colonel Drew. I'm not sure, for at that time I still had dysentery pretty bad, no pain just the constant drop, drop and uncomfortable sitting or walking and my bowels got weak and came out. I was in a kind of haze, just holding on and doing what had to be done. We got used to Colonel Drew after a while too and liked him. Captain Bernard, "C" Company's Captain, went off sick. He asked all the boys to go and see him in his dugout before he left. A good officer, well liked.

Sometime early in the fall, we finished our new firing line and went out one night and put up barbed wire in front of it. A few days after, the Worcester Regiment took over and, while they were in, the Turks stole all the wire. The Worcesters said we lost it and after that every time we met on the beaches there was a free for all. The 5th Royal Scots were good pals of ours. They even shared their rum ration with us until we got our own a few days after joining the Brigade. As the weather got colder, we had spells out to the beach a few days at a time and we began work on four dugouts to sleep in. I don't know how many men they would hold. About a hundred each I expect. We dug down about seven feet, then we put a ridgepole through it, then we put poles from side to side for beams and let them run in about six feet over the edge and covered them with three tiers of sandbags filled with earth. They were good and comfortable and warm.

We could not hear the sound of shells and we lay as close as we could. Dan Moore remarked the first morning that there would be nothing left but bones because when we were packed in there you hadn't room to turn or scratch and as soon as you got warm the lice had a great time. Our sergeant said "eat plenty, stow thick and be lousy!"

We just finished the new trenches and had one night in them when up comes the big rain storm and we were ordered to the trenches and did some grumbling and swearing. We did not know how lucky we were. The day before the storm on the Peninsula, it was up in November 1915, the heat about midday was dreadful. We lay down in the trench to get out of the glare of the sun. About four or five in the afternoon on the 27th of November the rain began the like I never saw and the thunder and lightning we never saw or heard before either. About nightfall a gale from the N.E. with rain sprang up and we had heavy freezing rain and snow for two days and nights. You could see miles and miles when a flash of lightning came and when 'twas over you could not see your hand before your eyes. We had to take hold of each other by the coattail to keep contact with one another. It came dark awful quick. When a flash of lightening came you could see to pick up a pin.

I was then out to the beach with Paddy Green from Pt. Verde, Jack Oakley of St. John's, Quartermaster Hector McNeil, Tom Harvey, and Chas Quick. We left to bring in the rations to our men as usual, but the Indian mule drivers did not want to go. The road was already in spots a raging river. So we had to get some English Officers to make them come. The Indian and gharry [A horse-drawn carriage, used primarily in Egypt and India, often as a cab] *I was guarding was the first to start. Just as we got under way he said he'd lost a shoe. He had kicked it off and thought he'd be sent back to camp, but no. The officer told him to drive on. We came to a river that was flooded, and he would not try to drive the mules. I tried to lead them, up to my waist in water, but there they stayed and would not budge, and*

the Indian would not try to drive them. At last I got vexed, and
from where I was spoking the wheel, I reached up and caught
the Indian and hauled him down and started whaling him, and
shoving him under. I do really believe I'd have killed him, I was
in such a rage at his stubbornness, only for an English officer
interfered and sent him back. I got up then and, between stabs
with the bayonet and yells, got the mules going, and so got our
grub in.

The rain turned to wet snow about midnight and then you
can imagine us—no underwear, pants to our knees, a gale of NE
wind and snow, wet to the skin and no shelter of any kind. And
when the rains came a dam the Turks had up in the hills burst
and flooded them and us out of our trenches. Many men died
that night, but not of our lot.

This account seems to be one instance in which Howard Morry's telling of the story fails to capture completely the horror of the actual event. Perhaps it was because, as he noted, the Newfoundlanders, being used to the cold, survived the incident without casualties. Others among the British and ANZAC forces were not so fortunate.

Howard Morry resumes his telling of the events in the aftermath of the storm:

Going in with the rations we had to pass around the corner of
a little hill before we came to the trenches and the Turks would
turn machine guns on it for about five minutes at a time and
then stop a minute or so. We always waited for the firing to
be over and then beat. While we were waiting our chance, I
thought I heard a moan, and went down to investigate, and
sure enough, there was a guy from the London Regiment lying
down on the wet ground. We walked him around for about five
minutes and warmed him up, showed him where to go for the
Red Cross hut and left him. Coming back we were under heavy
fire, we forgot about him. Next night while waiting for the usual
strafe to be over, we thought of him; he was still there but dead.

He must have laid down again just as we left and the rain killed him. Poor devil, he was never used to going out or knocking around in the cold. Always used to towns. Anyway he had not guts enough to live.

The last sentence appeared only in a later version of Howard's memoirs, written in the 1960s, not in the original version written in the 1940s. Whether the compassion exemplified in his earlier account of this episode hardened with time and later reflection, or whether he had always harboured the feeling that soldiers so ill-prepared to fend for themselves were not much more than a burden to themselves and a potential danger to their fellow soldiers is impossible to say.

When we came out after delivering the rations the night of the storm, CQMS Hector McNeil put me on guard duty on the dump where the rum had been stored. It was stacked in a ravine. But the flood coming down the valley from the salt lake struck the pile of boxes and drove them all over the valley. The rain was fierce, and the lightening would light up the whole country for miles around and, to make it more Hell, a Worcester Regt. man who had gone mad was staked out a short distance away and every yell out of him would almost scare the wits out of you.

The term "Post-Traumatic Stress Disorder" had not yet been coined in those days, and the term "Shell Shock" was only employed sporadically. In wwi, soldiers behaving in this manner were often treated as deserters or cowards and not considered victims. This poor unfortunate was lucky to have been treated even in this barbaric manner, rather than suffering the common penalty for abandonment of their post due to mental distress—a hasty court martial followed by the firing squad, in order to set an example to others. Two hundred and sixty-six British soldiers in wwi suffered this ultimate punishment. There is no record of any Newfoundlander being dealt with in this manner. Elsewhere in his memoirs, Howard Morry mentions witnessing such a court martial and execution, but the event most likely involved British rather than Newfoundland soldiers.

One of my trips back and forth around the dump I kicked over a box with two one gallon jars of rum in it. I picked it up and, when the lightening came, I saw what it was. It had been driven away up the hillside by the force of water when the dam burst. I wasn't long ripping the cover off with my bayonet. I was dead thirsty and it was cool and wet and, so I guess I took enough the first drink to quench my thirst as if it was water. I then filled my water bottle and put the rest of it under a big rock on the hill. By that time, the world was beginning to look a lovely place. No rain, or thirst, or lice, or anything. Quartermaster McNeil heard me singing, went into the dugout, and said to the fellows "Morry must be gone nuts. He's singing like a lark over there." He sent over Tom Harvey and Paddy Green from Pt. Verde to relieve me, but 'twas I relieved them when I produced the jar. They filled their water bottles, so I left them and went back to the dugout to sleep and dry my clothes. McNeil was a good trump and never turned me in, though he knew we'd got at the rum.

I had been sent out for a rest from the trenches a week earlier, as I was nearly through with dysentery. Every night four of us went in with a donkey and gharry with Indian driver with rations to the boys. It was a sticky job too as we were under fire practically all the time we were within range of the trenches, as they could hear the noise of the old iron gharries and keep firing at us. The very first night we were in I lost my driver. He was shot through the forehead while I was talking to him.

Mont Windsor was there also, and he brought out my letters to me. I lit a match to see who they were from. There must have been a sniper around for, fast as the match lit, the Indian got hit. He never stirred or spoke. Lights out for him was painless and swift. The next time, on a bright moonlit night, we lost all our mules, but not a man was hit. We lay behind the mules until almost day before the firing let up.

It may not be fair to speculate, looking at the circumstances from almost one hundred years after the fact, but one gets the sense that Howard felt little remorse or responsibility for the death of the Indian driver largely due to the common prejudices of the day. His manner of speaking about foreigners, somewhat edited for publication, leaves little doubt of the manner of thinking common to Howard and his peers at that time.

It seems to me that, from the night I got the first drink of rum, my dysentery began to improve. We always managed to secure lots of it after that and used it all the time to kill the impurities in the water. In about a fortnight I was almost well as ever. I told our doctor after about the cure and he said there might be something to it, he'd try it out. But he was killed next day at sick parade, as he was just pulling a tooth for one of our chaps, Willis White. Strange to say, though the shell burst quite near he never got a scratch.

We were sent out to the beach in squads during the day to help clean up rifles that were abandoned or turned in by soldiers being invalided home. We cleaned thousands. Of all the troops there, we came out of the storm good, only lost a few men. But the London Regt. that was with us only a few weeks, all went sick and were taken off. The morning after the storm we had to lie on top of the wet frozen ground behind piles of earth thrown up by the shell bursts, and behind bushes. Everything was in an awful mess. We had to hold practically all the line. A lot of our fellows were from the out harbours and bays and were used to hardship. The others lit small fires with coal sent in from the warships and they sat right in over them and got smoke blinded and colds. We kept away from the fires.

The Turks were coming over in droves. We kept firing at them and waving them back. We could have killed hundreds of them. But we really did not fire at them. We would fire fifteen rounds rapid, and then run our hands up and down the barrels to warm them. Ralph Goff and I were aback of a bush with some discarded great coats and things under us on the frozen ground. Ralph was cramped and was continually moving around, and Dave had said to him more than once, they are going to see you and you'll get hit. But poor Ralph could not keep still and finally got one in the backside right in the soft part, never hit a bone. We hauled down his pants and we had quite a time of it to get him bandaged, which we finally did, and he hauled himself back to the dressing station on the beach.

Things quietened down after a day or so. The trenches dried out, our clothes dried, the weather turned a bit warm again, and we got back in our trenches again and back to the old routine, except we had to hold about twice as much of the line as formerly, there were so many from the other Regiments gone sick. Every day General Cayley would come in the trenches and go through the line with a friendly word to everyone. He asked our officers if we could hold on a few more days, and of course they said yes, and we began to feel quite proud of ourselves, as well we might. I often think of those plucky kids, a lot of them between 18 and 20. I was only thirty-one and one of the oldest in the Regiment.

We began to think at this time that there was something on the move. There were certain hours of the night we were not allowed to fire a shot and the men that went away sick did not come back. We were also sent out between the lines night after night setting trip bombs for any Turk that would try to get to our trenches.

About this time, every morning at dawn, there would always be a few Turks coming over to surrender. They were dressed in rags, and some of them had sand bags tied around their feet.

The nights were awful long and lonely now. In spite of night patrols, etc., time began to hang. We were losing men with snipers and shell fire. We had to give up the peep hole we used to have at ground level through the parapets and had to use periscopes to look over, and they were always getting shot up.

We were losing a good many men by snipers. One Sunday, just before stand to (dusk) we were just about finished eating and a chap, Dunphy from St. John's or Placentia, was sitting right at the end of the traverse telling a yarn, when all of a sudden he stopped talking. One of the chaps said "what is wrong with Dunphy?" We looked and there he was dead with a biscuit in his hand. There was a big oak tree out front and the Turks kept firing at it and the glancing bullets came in the line. Once in a while they killed or wounded somebody. That night a few of us were detailed to go out and cut it down. Not a nice job, but no one got hit, and we did not get any more glancing bullets.

The names of us that were on patrol with Capt. Carter, without rifles, the night he got wounded: Ned Edgar, Jimmy Lang, Willis White, Mike Downey, Gravy Brown and I.

One sniper in particular was doing a lot of damage, but we could not find where he was hidden till, one day after rain, we saw him hanging out a bunch of washing on the bushes. That day it wasn't any trouble to get a chap to take your turn at the periscope. Everyone was watching to get a shot at him when he went to take in his wash. But just before dark we saw it disappear. He had a line around a bush and hauled it in and out that way. We went out that night and bombed him out of it. He was in a dugout covered all over with sods. He could not get out without help. We would not have found him, only he fired right in front of us. I don't know how he missed us. We threw some bombs in through the peep holes and killed him. Next night a few of us went out and tore up the dugout and got his sniper's rifle and two hundred rounds of ammunition. It was a dandy telescope sight and wind gauge, made in America by our good friends the Yanks, who were sucking the life blood out of Britain at that time, and for another year or more, till the Jerrys wiped their noses in the mud, and then they had to get in. I carried that rifle for miles and miles. Thought I'd get it home. I did pack and send it from the peninsula but it never did get home.

Time passed and the nights were long and cold, but it got warm in the middle of the day. Many of our chums were gone. Once we could stand on the fire step shoulder to shoulder. Now we were from twenty to fifty feet apart. Get up on the fire step, fire a shot, walk nine or ten steps, fire another. We passed the time at night watching for a flash from the Turkish lines, snap a shot at it, then get down and change position for another shot. At that time there were only about ten men for every thousand Turks.

I was feeling stranger and stranger; had letters from home telling me I was soon to be a daddy [Phyllis Mary Morry, born April 29, 1916]. A little more worry about Fredris my wife, who had just gone home [i.e., to Ferryland] from Edinburgh about five months. I was worried about how she'd make out.

All kinds of rumours going the rounds: we were going to be taken off and brought back to England for a refit; we were going to Mesopotamia; and we were going to Cape Helles, which was true. More and more of us were taken out every day and no replacements. Certain hours of the night, not to fire a shot, and spent a lot of time out in no man's land setting booby traps and trip bombs and rigging rifles in the line so they would go off at different times. We were beginning to feel the strain too. The line was very thinly held, and 'twas only a matter of some Turk coming over and getting in the trenches. Once they saw

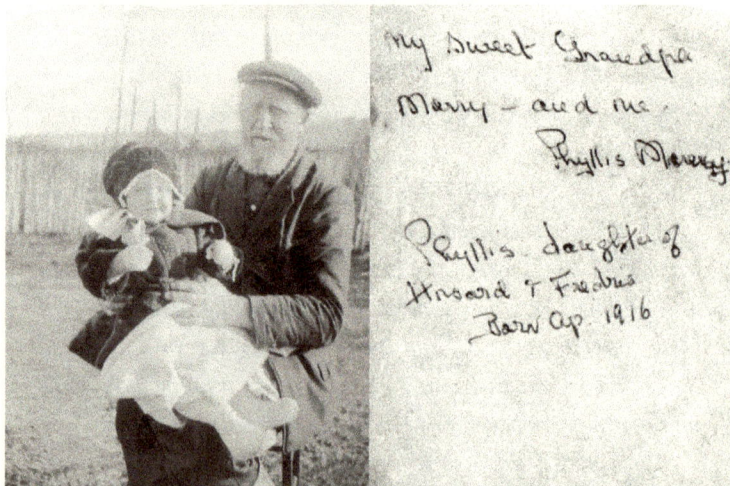

Howard Morry's father, Thomas Graham Morry, and first child, Phyllis, born in Newfoundland while Howard fought with the RNR on the Somme.

how thinly the line was held, 'twould be all over, for we had no
reserves to bring up. The last night came, at nightfall a lot of
the fellows were taken back. Only fifty left, me among them. At
midnight, Sunday, December 20th, 1915, twenty five of us were
taken back. That left just 25 in the line. And we all embarked
without the loss of a single man. I can't remember now what
officers we had or anything, but I do know that night when I
got on board of the ship, I got up in one of the boats and had a
real sleep.

Some sources give this date as December 9, 1915. It seems more likely that Howard's date is correct as the date of the departure since the time spent on Imbros (see next chapter) and the arrival at Cape Helles on Christmas Eve or thereabouts would not occupy the time from December 9 to 24.

Cape Helles Evacuation

The Royal Newfoundland Regiment had just played a pivotal role in one of the greatest deceptions in the history of warfare, managing to fool the Turks into thinking there remained a superior force in the trenches at Suvla Bay, all the time diminishing the ranks to a final low of twenty-five as the evacuation was completed, without the loss of a single man. But Suvla was only one of the beachheads held by the British and their allies, and there were others yet to be evacuated—Cape Helles amongst them. There can be little doubt that it was the success of the evacuation at Suvla Bay that led the general staff to choose the Newfoundlanders to take part in a similar evacuation ruse at Cape Helles. But the disappointment of the men, whose nerves were shattered by that first evacuation, to be chosen for another, only days later, must have been excruciating.

Incredibly, and for no apparent reason or at least none that was given, the official war diary of the RNR is interrupted after November 30, 1915, and does not resume once again until January 1, 1916. This means that the entire period of the evacuation at Suvla Bay, the time spent at Imbros, and the time spent in the trenches at Cape Helles before the evacuation is completely absent from this vitally important official record. At this time, the command of the RNR was transferred to Lieut. Col. A. L. Hadow (on December 6, 1915, according to G. W. L. Nicholson in *The Fighting Newfoundlander*) and, apparently, the missing month of records had something to do with this transfer of command. Nicholson also notes this confusion and states that the war office evidently neglected to inform the government of Newfoundland of the change in command or the reasons for it. Indeed, the Newfoundland government was still receiving communications from the former commanding officer, Lieutenant Colonel Burton, in reference to proposed promotions as late as December 24, 1915, though he himself was in hospital in Mudros at that time. Because of this lapse in record keeping during the change of command, the history of that period is entirely derived from secondary sources.

To Imbros Island we went from there and were disembarked and moved inland about three or four miles. The island was, for the most part, barren, with a few patches of land in the valleys. We were left to sleep where we could, but the officers had tents.

The days we spent on this island that fall were cold and miserable and the last day and night were especially bad. There was not a bush around, the wind NE, cold with heavy rain and we soaked to the skin. Three or four fellows would get together and, with their sheets and blankets and rifles, make a kind of tent that they could sit under and have a little shelter. Dan Moore, from Avondale, Harry Mifflin, and I went up in the hills and found a circular wall of rocks. It must have been a corral for sheep. We got in and laid our rifles across it, and hung our rubber sheets over them and, as it had come to blow, we weighted them down with rocks, and our lot compared with the rest of the poor devils that had not any shelter was much appreciated by us.

The conditions on Imbros reported by other authors, such as the information provided to G. W. L. Nicholson and evidently by Lieut.

Col. Hadow, differ markedly from what Howard Morry reports. Nicholson suggests, "For some thirty hours they enjoyed the unaccustomed comfort of hot food and shelter under canvas and most of all the blessed freedom from the strain of duty in the front-line trenches." A stark contrast to the actual conditions endured there by ordinary soldiers, and most likely more descriptive of the conditions enjoyed by the officers.

We dozed, and froze, and soaked in spots all night and, at 7 a.m. the following morning, we saw the Battalion forming up, so we made haste to join them, and found them finished breakfast and ready to march to the coast to embark again. It was still raining and cold and what we suffered no one can imagine who was not there. However, it cleared off at noon and we embarked a short time later. We got on a small steamer called the Red Breast *from Glasgow. We were so crowded in her that you stood as long as you could, then sat as long as you could. It was an awful long afternoon.*

After dark we pulled out. Rumours were flying round, but nothing definite. Some said we were going to Cape Helles. Others, we were going home to Newfoundland. I fell asleep sitting up against a stanchion on deck. I was awakened by a shell bursting quite near. "Cape Helles," I moaned, with my waking breath. And so it was.

Cape Helles—We landed there, before day on a Christmas eve, I think it was, or maybe a day or so before it. We were put in open dugouts with about a foot of water in them. The weather was cold and frosty some nights. We did not have any rations drawn and, though we were starving and lots of food in dumps there, we got very little for a few days till our order went through. A piece of Army red tape, and hard usage for a bunch of men worn out from months of trench warfare, exposure, and sickness.

On Christmas eve, a bunch (sixty) of us, were detailed to go on a digging party in charge of Sgt. Barrett. We had to go out to the beach to draw picks and shovels. We were fell out while the Sgt. went down in a dugout to see the English Major we were to get the tools from, and we were not long there when some of our fellows found out that there was a ration dump close by. We immediately raided it. It was a Headquarters dump with all kind of good things for the Officers (canned puddings, dates, Huntley and Palmer biscuits, prunes and even some bread, which we hadn't seen for months). I got a couple of loaves of soft bread, and filled the legs of my pants (we had been issued with long ones) with dates, a plum pudding canned, and all the other lads done alright too.

I guess we would have been alright and got away with it, only some of the fellows had filled sand bags with stuff. Barrett came back and fell us in two deep; when he gave us a right turn he noticed something bulky on one of the men's backs, Jellico Walsh (now Doctor Walsh). He had found a sand bag and filled it with good things unfortunately for us. He immediately ordered us to be searched. Fortunately for the most of us, a cloud came over the moon and we got a chance to dump our swag. You'd hear the thumps of bread, plum puddings, potted chicken, ham, etc., behind us in the grass.

We were marched back and put under arrest. Next morning, Christmas Day, we were brought before the general and the old major read the charge against us. Gen. Cayley, however, stood our good friend. He said, "don't you think it's against human nature to fall out a bunch of starving men on top of a ration dump and expect them not to eat it?" So we got off with a reprimand. I can still see the twinkle in old Cayley's eye as he dismissed us.

That day two Turkish airplanes bombed us and, as that was the first time we were bombed, we did not like it one bit. They killed four officers with one bomb in the afternoon, down by the YMCA hut. We got three army biscuits and a Dixie of Bully Stew each for our dinner. We did not do any trench duty there; we were too sick—we had an attack of Jaundice there. More than half the fellows got it and it was pitiful to see them as yellow as guinea pigs. A good many died. I did not get it, but practically everyone did.

Before I go any further I must tell you of the treatment we got for dysentery and jaundice. For dysentery, I'd fall in on sick parade, get a needle in the arm and an egg cup full of castor oil (ugh!), which I was taking for weeks, and it only made me worse. After a while I'd keep it in my mouth until I got outside the hospital, till one day the doctor saw me getting rid of it and called me back and gave me another egg cup full. Always after that he asked me a question after he gave me the oil and I had to swallow it before I could answer him. Then he'd say no bully beef, no stew, no bacon, which was all we got. We were supposed to get bread, milk, oatmeal and other food but, whoever got it, we did not. The same applied to the jaundice patients. They looked horrible; their eyes were as yellow as saffron, and so was their skin.

I forgot to mention how bad our men were with dysentery, jaundice and fever, and still on active duty, while at least one of our doctors at home were turning conscripts down as physically unfit for from $25 and up.

One night we were sent digging and Soper was detailed to come with us. When we got out there he looked so bad, the Sgt. and some of the fellows made a comfortable place for him to lie down. When we were coming in I went to get him. I shook him, thought he was asleep, but he was gone. We brought him in. First we thought he had been shot, but no, he just pegged out poor fellow [records indicate 29 December, 1915].

We were still on short rations, but we found a means of fixing that. At night we'd get past the guards and go out to the beach where the English Regiments had a bakery. We were not getting any soft bread. We'd follow the truckloads of bread and, when there'd be a burst of fire, the drivers would generally stop and seek shelter. Then we'd climb on board and dump off a lot of bread and pick it up when they had gone. We also got some

dates. I remember giving a loaf of bread and some dates to Sgts.
Greene and Barrett one night after a successful raid. The Turks
were shelling like hell and the four or five of us who went out
that night got all we could carry.

Sadly, Sgts. Walter Greene and Harold Barrett, who both eventually attained the rank of Lieutenant and were decorated for valour
(Greene receiving the Distinguished Conduct medal at Caribou Hill
in Gallipoli and Barrett the Military Medal at Gueudecourt), were
also to both die in battle, Barrett on August 16, 1916, at Ypres and
Greene on November 20, 1917, at Marcoing. Greene had played a
part in facilitating Howard Morry's wedding by turning a blind eye
when he discovered him AWOL.

After a few weeks there, the evacuation started. One afternoon a
Scottish Regt. made an attack up the hill and we had a ringside
seat for about an hour. They were repulsed with heavy losses.

Next day we got orders to go to the beach, we had to cross
about two miles of open country, exposed to the shell and shrap-
nel fire of the Turks. There were not many of us left there then,
about three hundred I should think. We went off at fifty yards
distance, one group of five or six at a time, six paces apart. We
had two miles to go over exposed ground, before we got over the
hill out of sight. While we were waiting for our turn, we watched
those who went before us. We'd see shells burst around them
everywhere, then you would not see them with dust and smoke
for a while. The shrapnel was also bursting overhead. Then it
came to our turn and away we went. There were lots of shells
bursting all around us but we did not have one casualty.

When we were leaving, Capt. Rowsell gave me a bag with 48
tins of Maconochie rations to bring along, with all my own gear.
He must have thought I was a mule to give me that extra weight,
especially as I was just getting over the dysentery. Anyway our
Sergeant gave us an order to double, to get out of shellfire, and
I managed to lose the rations in the bustle. I never was asked

about them afterwards. Rowsell must have forgotten about them. I often wonder what Rowsell thought I was and why did he not give the rations among the bunch. He did the same thing when we were leaving the trenches in Suvla. He gave me a box of 75 pounds of rifle cartridges to bring along with my other gear, but I only brought that to the first big shell hole we came to, where I accidentally, on purpose, fell into the hole and left the ammunition there. I also forgot to mention that before we left Suvla, we spent days and days digging and burying Bully Beef and ammunition in shell holes, so there was really no reason for me to bring that ammo out to the beach.

When we got out to the beach we were put in dugouts formerly occupied by Greek labourers, and they were actually alive with fleas. The cold weather seemed to have put an end to the lice, but the fleas were worse. The dugouts were in the face of the cliff and were exposed to the guns from Anzac where the Aussies had evacuated. They were in tiers, one above the other.

Cape Helles British Headquarters.

The roof of the lowest made a walk in front of the others. There were three tiers of them. We worked regular shifts then loading ammo and stuff on board the steamers laying alongside the River Clyde, which ship, along with several others, were sunk to make a harbour.

There were other gangs loading the officers' stores and when we were detailed for that purpose we were delighted and lived like kings for a week or so. There were oil stores there and tons of oil. We managed to sneak a few of them to our dugouts. They were not being taken off anyway and there was flour and raisins, baking powder etc. We managed to get quite a supply of it and had many a meal of pancakes. There were lots of canned meats, hams etc. biscuits and cases of whisky—hundreds of cases of it—piled near there. Our fellows were put to guard it where we were billeted. We had to go up over the hill and about a couple of hundred yards back in a ravine to get at the stuff. When the Tommys were on guard it was no go, but as soon as our fellows took over we went every night came back loaded with good things and a few bottles of whisky a man (which we used with discretion).

We began to get strong and hearty and fat again, and the officers were quite a while before they found out that some of our fellows were half drunk to work during the day, so they put the Limeys back on guard again. But we got around that. About twenty of us would go at a time and while two or three kept the guard busy the rest would get to work and grab everything in sight. There were lots of riding breeks [cavalry trousers normally worn exclusively by officers] *there, and soon some of our boys were sporting them.*

Then at last some of our chaps got so bad they were always drunk two or three of them, and we were detailed to go break all the whisky bottles. About a dozen of us were sent with an English officer for every three. We had to open the cases take out the bottles and break them one by one, but still we managed to save a few, leave them in the case or cover them with glass. But it was only a few we saved and that night we went back and salvaged them and brought them out and dug holes in the floors of our dug outs and hid them there. At night we'd take one out for three or four fellows and have a little singsong. There were lots of cigarettes too, which we were delighted to get. One morning some of the lads found that the bakery ovens were left full of bread, cookies etc. They were long ovens about 10 of 12 ft. long. I crawled in one and saw a tray of buns in the inside of it, and I crawled out backwards, when lo and behold here was an English Colonel with his orderly to take them, so I had to be content with some nice fresh bread, and as we had lots of good butter also from the Officers Canteen, we were well away.

Incidentally, while we were at Suvla, we never saw butter for months, and then we got a pound can between 5 men for a week, we generally put the lot between two army biscuits and ate it the one meal. The difference between the Officers' food and that of other ranks was a crying shame and a disgrace to any army, but that is how it was on the Peninsula.

The Turks had a big gun, Asiatic Annie, right across the straits from us, which was firing intermittently day and night. We had a man on watch and, when he saw the flash or smoke, you had while you could count 27 to make shelter. There were holes dug all along the front of the cliff for that purpose. We were under a big cliff and had shelter from rifle fire, but we were exposed to shell fire from across the Straits and from Anzac Cove, where the Turks moved down when the Aussies evacuated it. We lost a few men with shell fire from Anzac Cove. They only fired a few shells a day, about twenty or so, but never did much damage, so we soon got tired of running for shelter.

One afternoon I was cookhouse orderly for the day and was speaking to Bob Morris the Company's cook. He was in a cook house only about ten feet away from ours. We were swapping the latest "latrine official," going back to England to refit etc., when we heard the big one coming. I threw myself down, but

Bob never ducked and he lost his head as a result of a direct hit with a big shell. He was killed instantly.

About a half hour afterward, we were told to get ready to leave at nightfall. In the meantime, I, with a half dozen others, were told off to bury poor Bob. I thought then what hard luck he had to be killed just before we left. I had reason to change my mind lots of times afterwards. We went off to bury him. There was a large open pit there. Three privates were buried together. The pit was filled from one end in a kind of a slope and the privates were buried one above the other. One sergeant was buried. There was clay between each and lime chucked in. There must have been hundreds buried in that pit. By the time we had Bob buried we hurried back to our dugouts and found our men fell in and ready to march on board.

On January 3, 1916 we got orders to draw a week's rations and we had to go around a corner of a hill where there was a crossroad which was always under fire. On the morning of the 3rd, Hal Roper and I were detailed among others to go to two big iron tanks that were there, one about a hundred yards away from the other, one on a hill and the other one right beside the crossroad. There was a sentry box on the side of the road right by the nearest tank, and Hal and I just stopped there to decide which one we'd go to when the shelling started up. We heard a big one coming and we both ran and threw ourselves down on the ground. It burst right where we were standing, and blew a hole about 10 yards across. It was quickly followed by half a dozen more, but when the first one burst I scrambled under the tank that was nearest me, and stayed there for about an hour till things had quieted down. Then I filled my two pails and went back. No sign of Roper. I thought the first shell had got him. So I reported to Capt. Summers, that Roper was killed. Why, he said, Roper came in here about 10 minutes ago and said you were blown up. That shelling shook me up quite a bit.

All next day troops were marching down that road and were getting knocked off if they were unfortunate enough to be there when the shelling was on. I made three trips around it to draw rations, and the fourth time I asked Capt. Summers to excuse me, that I was almost a wreck, which he did. We got all our rations without losing a man. That night after dark I was sent to draw a case of milk, and when I went up to the dump, a Scot was on guard at the entrance of a dugout they had built under the huge pile of cases of milk, beef, etc. He said go down and see the officer, when I went down they were celebrating Burns night. I stayed to hear a few Scotch songs and to drink a health to Burns, and started off for the dugouts.

When I came to the corner, there was an English Regt. marching out. They had to quit during the night on account of the shell fire. Just as I laid down the milk to take a rest while the bunch was passing, the shelling started. I heard the officer giving the order to scatter and get for the beach. When I heard the first one burst, then the moans of the wounded, I rushed out and grabbed a man and brought him in, and I heard another groan. I was scared to death but I rushed out and fell over the chap, who was moaning, and brought him in. He was saying over and over "Oh my poor wife and children." The officer, a Sub, was yelling his head off for me to bandage him up. He told me he had a flash light in his haversack so I got it out and had a look. He was hit in the shoulder badly. I heard the other chap groan again, and I went to have a look at him, and I knew it was all over with him, he had it in the chest. The officer said he had a flask of brandy, so I got it out for him, and he took a big drink, while I was trying to bandage him. Then he said give that chap a drink and see what you can do for him, so I gave it to the poor fellow, but he was too far gone. Then the officer began to yell for stretcher bearers, and I gave him another pull at the flask. He said "have one yourself and get me out of this." "Sir," I said, "I've got to report back with milk I was sent for," and he got mad as hell anyway. I got him to his feet, and took the case of milk under my other arm. But after going about 20 yards, I found I could not do two things at once. So I left the milk and helped

*him along. In a couple of minutes the stretcher bearers came
and took him. I got the milk and went on to report.*

*We were in full marching order, as we had to go straight on
board. On the way to the ship I gave my ankle an awful wrench
and had to fall out. They went off and the Capt. told me to follow on as fast as I could. I was suffering great pain and could
just limp along. When I got to the embarking place, the loading officer told me I had to go to "V" Beach where the French
troops embarked. It was no use in me telling him that I was to
go on board there, the steamer* River Clyde*. That is where all
our troops went off.*

The River Clyde *is where the British and* ANZAC *forces had
made the initial landing almost a year before, in April 1915.
She was loaded with troops, and at nightfall she pretended to
break down and drifted toward the shore. The Turks thought
they had a great prize, as the soldiers were all kept out of sight,
and the Turks allowed her to drift ashore without firing upon
her. When she struck, the British troops all rushed ashore and
made a landing. Afterwards, the British ran six more ships
ashore there stem to stern, and made a harbour out of it. Small
ships brought ammunition and stores on her outside, and were
landed through her, and that is where all our troops got off.*

*Well to get on, I started off for "V" Beach along the shore for
about 2 miles. And I sweated with pain and anxiety, as I never
saw one man on the way, and the Turks were pouring shells on
it. I guess they'd had an inkling something was cooking. When I
got there I found it deserted, and had to start right back again.
Only this time, it was quite bright, as some of their shells had
hit one of our dumps and it was burning fiercely, and lit up the
whole beach. It's a good thing the hill sheltered the place where
the British Troops were moving off.*

*When I got back, I reported to the officer, who would not
believe me. I was sure mad. He told me to go in the bunk hole
and wait to go aboard with the last lot. I made several attempts
to mingle with the crowd, as I did not want to get astray from*

the Battalion, but each time he spotted me and sent me back. At last, I gave it up and went in and fell asleep. By and by the last bunch was going and someone woke me up and I went aboard. It was getting pretty rough and the wharves were smashing up, and me being quite lame now, I decided to dump my pack and equipment or I'd never make it. So I took it off and pitched it in the sea and had all I could do to board the ship. I don't know what ship it was. I heaved a great sigh of relief when I got on board the destroyer. There were a lot of French and British troops on her. I went below and got in a bunk and a RAMC fellow tied up my foot and gave me a couple of pills, and I tell you I slept!

We lay off there and, in the morning, the destroyer shelled the ration dumps and set them all on fire. The Turks began pouring down to the beach, but the ships soon put an end to their advance and they kept them back till all the dumps were all destroyed; what a waste that was. I think it was the 8th or 9th of January we left Cape Helles.

In actual fact, the loading officer was right; the Newfoundlanders were scheduled to embark at "V" Beach on lighters that would ferry them to the destroyer waiting to carry them to Mudros Island, via Imbros. The first group of Newfoundlanders went out on January 7, 1916, another on January 8 and Howard's group on January 9. Had he been able to rejoin his group he would have travelled with them on board the HMS *Mars*. But, due to his ankle injury and his slow progress, Howard must have missed them at "V" Beach and had to return to where the *River Clyde* was careened in order to depart with other British and French troops. As he notes below, he did not rejoin the Newfoundlanders for several days and was thus amongst the last of them to leave the area for Alexandria on the HMT *Nestor* on January 12, 1916.

These two evacuations were hard on the nerves. I never woke for hours and hours. We landed on Imbros or Mudros Island. I don't know which. I stayed with a French battalion that night and next

*two days I spent with Highland regiments till I found out where
our boys were camped. I was told where to find them on the third
morning and set off quite light, as my pack was gone with blanket
and rubber sheet etc., just had my web equipment and rifle. Got
to the battalion about 2 p.m. and found a bit of mail for me.*

Among Howard Morry's many scrapbooks, notes, and memorabilia concerning the RNR in WWI, I found a poem in typed mimeograph form concerning the time spent on the Peninsula. The name of the clever writer is unfortunately not revealed, whether deliberately (to avoid incurring the wrath of the brass) or simply out of humility. It may be that it was composed by many, each contributing a stanza as the events unfolded (note the poem's title misspells Suvla Bay, but this was a common occurrence in the writings of the men). Since I have not seen it published elsewhere, I am adding it to Dad Morry's narrative to indicate that his experiences and feelings were shared by many at the time:

*1ˢᵗ Newfoundland Regiment at Sulva Bay, 1915-1916
(Anonymous)*

*When this bloody war is over
Oh how happy we will be,
When we start our homeward journey
To Newfoundland o'er the sea.*

*Oh how dearly we loved Sulva;
When we landed in the Bay,
Till the Turks with shrapnel found us
Took our Adjutant away.*

*Then we moved into a Nulla,
Somewhat further from the Beach,
When the high explosives found us;
Though we seemed far out of reach.*

Next we moved into an area,
Called reserved by the Brigade;
We learnt the rules of Sanitation
That were by Major Hadow made.

Next we moved into the Trenches,
Right into the firing line;
And we stood upon the fire steps
But the Turks we saw no sign.

Then our "guts" got out of order,
And the Dysentry [sic] came;
To De-Lisle we all are running,
Every day was just the same.

Next our eyes and skin got yellow
Our "discharge" was Pink and Red;
It scared us all so very badly,
It's "Jaundice" now the boys all said.

How the flies did daily chase us,
Straight from the "Latrine" they came
Do a two step in our "Jam-tin",
And invade our 'tot' of rum.

How we miss our former Colonel,
He will climb these hills no more;
May he find another Bullet,
Far away on England's shore.

Twas now that General Cayley set us,
To include within his line;
The hill that Caribou we christened,
Don't you think we did it fine?

If the "Bloody" Turk attacks us,
Would we scatter to the rear;
Would we leave our pals and beat it,
I don't think, no "Bloody" fear.

We will stick them with the Bayonet,
We will shoot them down like fun;
If we beat them, then you'll hear us,
Let's get at the "Bloody" Hun.

Captain Wilson says we're dirty,
Armstrong's views are just the same;
But we never are downhearted,
What is dirt compared to Fame?

All our lousy shirt out Jam tins,
O'er the parapet we throw;
Do the staff complain about us?
No they chucked it long ago.

When we all are feeling hungry,
Thoughts to "Iron Rations" go;
Shall we all ask leave to eat them?
No, we ate them long ago.

Should the Turks with gas attack us,
There is nothing to be feared;
If we use our respirators,
But they too have disappeared.

When from Sulva we were ordered,
To evacuate our lines;
We refused to leave our Trenches,
Till we sent up many lives.

And the Turks when they came over,
Up into the air they went;
For our bombs and mines exploded,
Just exactly what we meant.

Then we sailed across to Imbros,
One day there we had our rest;
Then they sent us to "Cape Helles",
Why they did, God knows best.

In the dark they let us wander,
There was no one sent to meet;
Till we found some empty dugouts,
There we rest our weary feet.

Aeroplanes dropped bombs upon us,
Shells went screaming overhead;
Cover from the "Iron" was asked for,
There is none the staff all said.

Then for Christmas cheer they gave us,
Bully Beef and Biscuits few;
No Tobacco, Rum or Whiskey,
Did we grumble? Wouldn't you?

Then they sent an order for us,
In the night to send our boys;
For Pick and Shovel from Headquarters,
Food they pinched and made a noise.

They brought back no "Bloody" shovels,
And I fear the story's true;
For they raided and stole Puddings,
Pinched the General's Turkey too.

Then unto the beach they sent out,
To replace the dirty Greeks;
Where mid shells we loaded lighters,
And no cover did we seek.

Other jobs they also gave us,
Digging graves and chopping wood;
Canteen guard they made us furnish,
So we looted all we could.

Then like Sulva, we left Helles,
Came to Suez for a rest;
All day long the Colonel drilled us,
For the General thought it best.

And the order came to dress up,
For the Trenches made us slack;
So we bought some fancy clothing,
But were told to take it back.

When this "Bloody" war is over,
Oh, how happy we shall be;
No fatigues and no more fighting;
Then we really shall be free.

Will go back to Terra Nova,
To the Girl we left behind;
At Placentia, or in Glenwood,
What her name is, never mind.

Back in Egypt

The histories of the Royal Newfoundland Regiment neglect to offer an adequate explanation for why the troops were sent back to Egypt after the evacuation from Gallipoli. It certainly wasn't for R&R after the hardships endured on the Peninsula and at Cape Helles, as the following account makes clear. Nor could it have been considered as further training for the campaign that followed, since the conditions in Egypt could hardly prepare the troops for the horrors awaiting them in France and Belgium. Camp Zagazig was of strategic importance to the British as it guarded the entrance to the Suez Canal and, in fact, between January 26 and February 4, 1915, exactly one year before the arrival of the Newfoundlanders there, the British forces stationed at Zagazig had to fend off an attack by the German and Ottoman army, intent on seizing control of the canal. But that attempt was frustrated, and there was little or no threat of a recurrence a year later. G. W. L. Nicholson, in his masterful history of the regiment, *The Fighting Newfoundlander*, suggests they were sent there for "reconditioning" prior to redeployment in France. But that makes little sense, since the conditions were in no way similar to those faced in France. He may simply be repeating the official explanation provided by officers involved in the deployment. In the end, it may just be one more example of questionable decision making by a high command out of touch with the conditions of the soldiers in the field.

That night I went on board a destroyer and from that to a big ship. I slept like a log, on the deck. We were taken back to Egypt again. I don't remember anything much about it, the ship's name, or what kind of a ship, if it we stopped at Alex or not, but I remember going thru the Suez Canal and landing at Port Tawfik.

The next few months are a kind of blank to me. I guess it was from being so sick and so much shelling and under a strain all the time. Spots I can remember, but the rest is blank.

When we landed in Port Tawfik we were sent about 16 miles in the desert to a station called Zagazig. We would go out to Port Tawfik once every two or three days. Most of us did not bother, as there was not much to see and we did not have much energy anyway. We stayed there for a month or two. I'm not sure how long, we were drilled every day, we got a new Colonel, Hadow an Indian Army man, a real martinet. I guess he thought we were Indians, anyway we thoroughly hated him. We did a twelve mile march every day in the heat of the sun, and were not allowed to bring our water bottles. We missed our old Colonel Burton, who came out with us and got wounded and left us on the Peninsula. He knew us and liked us and we him. Our good friend, General Cayley, was also away from us. He always took our part.

Actually, Hadow had been nominally in charge from before the time of the evacuation at Cape Helles, but in the chaos that ensued, the troops may not have been entirely aware of the change of command. They simply knew that Colonel Burton was injured and gone for now. G. W. L. Nicholson suggests that, although Hadow was rough on the men, his toughness prepared them for what they had yet to face in France and Belgium. Nicholson also suggests that "fair-minded Newfoundland veterans would come to give as their considered opinion: 'Colonel Hadow made the Regiment." However it must be remembered that Nicholson relied upon Hadow as his advisor while writing his history, since Hadow was one of the few surviving officers from the Regiment. Since Nicholson gives no references to support this statement, it must be considered open to question. Certainly it does not conform with Howard Morry's opinion, often stated in written and spoken word over a lifetime. Also of note is the fact that Hadow only commanded the regiment over a two year period from late in 1915 until late in 1917, during which time he was absent on what was described as stress leave (presumably PTSD) in Britain for lengthy periods of several months on at least two occasions. To credit him with responsibility for "making the Regiment" is to do a disservice to the other officers that served as commander before and after him and during his absences, as well as those more junior officers who stayed with the men until the end of hostilities or until their deaths.

While we were here, our mail and parcels from home arrived, and we lived good for a while. We got lots of nice things; chocolate bars, butter, cakes, homemade jam, all kind of eatables and smokes. But here again we got a raw deal, as there were only about 300 of us left, and the parcels for the whole Battalion (1060) were there in a pile. Our own parcels were gone after a week or so. Even though we had letters from our pals back in hospital telling us to take their parcels, the officers would not give them to us, and they were there spoiling in the sun. There was much grumbling and grousing. But we still got orders to leave them alone, and they put a guard on them. But, of course, it was the Cape Helles story over again. Every night, after Lights Out, a chap or two from each tent went to the dump and came back loaded. The Sentry would conveniently turn his back. We ate what we could, and buried the rest for the next day. The pile soon began to diminish and the officers who, for the most part, were good trumps, did not take any notice of the shrinkage and, by the time we left, there was not much left.

One night, a chap in our tent, Gladney by name, proposed to steal a few bottles of whiskey from the officers. They had one marquee for eating in, and one for the mess stores. Gladney had been orderly in the Officers' mess the preceding day and said it was no trouble to get a few bottles if one fellow would watch and give the alarm if any one came around. There were Edmund Edgar, Dan Costello, Walter Thomas, Jack Davis and I, in our camp. And we debated for hours about it, as it was a serious thing, and, if we were caught, we'd get an awful soaking. At last we decided to draw lots, and it fell to me to go with him. We went and stood in the shadow of some tents, watching the proceedings through the door of the officers' marquee. The dinner was over and they were standing up drinking a toast when Gladney rushed in to the marquee where the stores were. Gladney seemed to me to be an age in there. Suddenly, I saw an officer, Lieut. Nunns, get up and come out of the marquee. I gave the signal, but no sign of Gladney. Lieut. Nunns went in. The next thing I heard was a shout, and I beat it for our tent. Got in and we blew the light out, and we all pretended to be asleep. Gladney came in a minute after me. He was just coming out when Lieut. Nunns came in so he ran to the end of the marquee, pulled out his knife and ripped a big hole in the back of it and got away before he was caught. He buried the four bottles of whiskey in the sand where we could find it when things quieted down.

About 10 minutes after, one of the guard came and woke us up; of course he had a job to wake us. They went around to all camps and found there was no one missing. So it was blamed on men from some of the other Battalions. We drank their health a few nights afterwards. Watty [Walter Davis] *and Gladney were killed in France; also Edgar. Dan Costello died years ago. But I think Jack Davis is still alive.*

The next day an incident occurred that could have had serious consequences. The Ghurkha troops were camped near us and we and the Aussies got very friendly with them. So friendly that, when the Egyptians who ran the canteen there charged us too much, they raided them and got in trouble for our sake. Some of them were tied to gun wheels and left in the sun with their hands tied behind them. Pretty cruel we thought, because the flies were thick all over them. Some of our fellas slunk down and cut them clear and were caught doing it, and four of our boys were tied with them next day. Back of our lines we did not know till we came off parade. Then some of our lads saw an officer from the Worcester Regt. taking a snap of them. We protested to the officers but 'twas no use. Kings Regs.

They immediately sent the word around and we all went to our officers and protested it was inhumane treatment, for the sun and the flies had them nearly crazy. The officers didn't know what to do, as the Colonel had gone on 10 days leave just a few minutes before. While we were debating about it someone cut them clear.

Then we got a round-robin and got every man's name on it and sent it in to headquarters, asking for the removal of Hadow. We did not get any answer to it. But after he came back he was a different man.

After that, we had a song about him and sang it on all route marches, and he hated our guts, but there was not a thing he could do about it. He surely heard it, but he never pretended to hear it. Our officers got a great kick out of it. In fact some of them always got us to sing it.

I can remember only the first verse now:

I'm Hadow
Some Laddo
I just came off the Staff
I'm in charge of the first Newfoundlanders
They know it not half
I'll march them. I'll drill them
I'll make the Beggars sweat
I'm Hadow
Some Laddo
I'll be a general yet

We got clear of him after the July drive.

We were a close knit bunch; back one another up in every-thing when we were on patrol or any kind of do. You could depend on your chums on your right and left not to let you down or to fall back and leave you in the lurch. I'll bet there never was a bunch of soldiers since the world began so united. It was share and share alike. Some of our boys with a bunch of Aussies got into some kind of scrape one Sunday afternoon in Port Tawfik. I remember a bunch of us were lying around reading and writing etc. when one of our boys rushed in and said "scatter boys, there's a helluva a do on in Port Tawfik between our boys and the Aussies and the British troops and they are sending in for help." This chap was from the orderly room when the order came, and he beat it to spread the news right away, and we made ourselves scarce in a hurry. 'Twas an awful racket while it lasted, and we were lucky to be out of it, as there were lots of broken limbs and lengthy punishment out of it.

Here is the Australians farewell to Egypt:

Land of heat and sweaty socks
Gonorrhoea, syph and pox
The black man's heaven
The white man's hell
Bastard Egypt, fare you well

The Aussies, as well as the rest of us, hated the gyppos, as we called them.

We Newfies in the Regt. stuck together and now, after thirty three years, when we meet and shake hands, we feel a thrill. Last summer I met a chap, Jack St. John. I had not seen for thirty years. The tears came to his eyes when we shook hands. We yarned for two full hours about the old days. When we were parting he said "Howard, there was never a bunch like us and never will be again."

We left there sometime in March [March 14, 1916, on board the HMT *Alaunia*] *and got on board of a big ship and went back through the canal. While we were waiting to board her, we were much interested in watching the loading of camels for the Mesopotamia campaign. So off we go, and we thought of the rest we were going to have on shipboard. Sez you! Every day we had kit inspection about four times a day, short arm inspection for venereal disease every day* ["short arm" being the soldiers' euphemism for penis], *boat drill and, if that was not enough, old Hadow had us marching around the deck one hour in the morning and one in the afternoon. At first we marched with our boots on, but on the third day we had to march in our bare feet. The result—we nearly all got sore feet or flat or blistered feet. Imagine that treatment for men who had suffered and sweated for almost a year. Instead of giving us a week's rest, he kept us right at it. Many were the curses bestowed on Hadow. So after a few days, much to his disgust, the doctor advised him to discontinue the march.*

In *The Fighting Newfoundlander*, Nicholson states, "a sixty minute route march around the decks every day helped keep all ranks in condition." Reading Howard Morry's account above, we can see once again how very different were the points of view of senior officers and enlisted men. Nicholson seems to have been completely unaware of the negative impact these route marches had on the soldiers, both physically and mentally, though one would assume he had access to the doctor's logs and would have known about this, had he researched them. It seems likely he relied entirely on the testimony of Hadow when writing about this event. One can imagine that, as his principal advisor in writing this book, Lt.-Col. Hadow would not have provided him with the additional details given by Howard Morry and would not have given any suggestion of the impact of his orders on the men.

France—Preparations for
the July Drive

Having departed Egypt, common sense would have dictated that the troops be adequately equipped en route for the climatic conditions they were about to contend with in France. Not so. As Howard Morry makes clear, the commanders responsible for the RNR's preparations before the Battle of the Somme had made no provisions for allowing the men to change into kit suitable for the cold, wet conditions that would plague them in the trenches. Call it lack of planning or obliviousness to the needs of the men under their command, whatever it was, once again the troops on the line fell victim to poor leadership.

We disembarked, in Marseilles. What a place! And what girls! They looked real good to us after Egypt and the Dardanelles. There were big high gates at the end of the wharf with long iron bars, and the girls on one side and our boys on the other got in a lot of kissing, etc., through the bars, before the officers got wise. I was one of four detailed to go with the sergeant to the prison there to bring in four deserters from the Dublin fusiliers to our train. The girls in hundreds just out of the factories mobbed us. "Souvenir, souvenir" is all you could hear, or maybe a pair of bare arms and a breast against you when a girl got a chance to get a real hug and kiss at you. Needless to say, we did not get far, and the sergeant decided to try and get back to the wharf again, minus our cap badges, shoulder badges, buttons and anything moveable we had on us. We were lucky to be able to hold on to our bayonets and rifles, as one of the boys had his braces and belt and all his trenching tools taken, and had to use one of his hands to hold up his trousers. We finally got back, and Donnelly read the riot act to us. We said nothing. We were glad to be back behind the gates again away from those lovelies, and we had the pleasure of seeing Capt. Donnelly going out with a detail of six and he waving his stick. Somehow it seemed to frighten them for a bit, and he made good headway till a lovely girl, threw her arms around him and was doing a good job of kissing him while the others cleaned him of his cap badge, equipment and all. His men, no doubt profiting from our experience, did not turn up for three days and were the envy of us all for weeks to come, and did their punishment with perpetual grins on their faces. Donnelly—well I don't know; sometimes the privates have the best of things.

We were put in cattle cars and brought to the north of France. We were packed so tight in those loathed cars that we'd stand as long as we could, and then sit. Stop three times a day for a meal. It was cold weather in the north. After I don't remember how long, but after some days and nights, we were dumped off in a deserted village (I've forgotten the name of) [Buigny l'Abbé] at twelve o'clock p.m. in about four inches of snow, to take shelter where we could—old barns without door or windows and leaky roofs, no fires. We had our khaki drill with knee pants, one shirt, no underwear and, after the heat of Egypt, to be dumped off in the snow. We got into an old barn and hauled some old straw together and kept warm. Next day we got issued with warm clothes. It's a wonder we did not all die of exposure. But, strangely enough, we had very few sick.

In the morning we started off for the front line. We marched as far as Louvencourt and our billets were there for a few

days. Then we moved to Beaumont Hamel, Mailly-Maillet,
Englebelmer and Acheux. We began to bring in shells at night,
drilled and got acquainted with gas and used to our gas masks,
and fire from Stokes guns, liquid fire, etc. and all the other hor-
rors of modern war so we would not get scared when we were up
against the real thing.

In *The Fighting Newfoundlander*, Nicholson reports that during this time small numbers of officers "and other ranks" were permitted the privilege of leave in Britain. This report is not verified in any other records of the Regiment's movements, and it does not appear to be the case from Howard Morry's account of events. It is possible Nicholson broadened out the fact that officers were accorded such a privilege and mistakenly assumed the same opportunity was afforded to enlisted men. The official records reveal that it was not until the war was more than three years old and almost over that enlisted men who had been with the Regiment from the beginning were permitted leave in Britain or even at home in Newfoundland in some cases. It remains highly unlikely that men who had been in the field of war for less than a year, and who were not generally treated with undue solicitousness by their new commanding officer, would have been accorded this privilege. However, it is known, and this is reported by Nicholson, that Hadow was himself in Britain, at this time, being awarded the CMG by the King, evidently in recognition of his services in Gallipoli, though he only arrived there for the evacuation.

I'll always remember the first night we went in the trenches
in France. It was night, snowing a little and freezing and, to
make it worse, about 18 inches of water in the trenches with
the scum of ice at the top. By the time we slugged in to our part
of the line, we were chilled to the bone. No one can imagine the
sufferings in the trenches, wet to the knees and cold, standing
in freezing water up to our knees, then get up on the fire step
for a while. Your feet would warm up a bit. We stood on the

fire step looking over, two together; one changed each half hour to make sure none of the sentries would fall asleep. For I can tell you, when one was properly weary, you'd be standing there leaning on the parapet watching the star shells and flares with occasional shellfire or a burst of rifle and machinegun fire, if either side thought they saw something move on no-man's-land; still if things quieted for a few minutes you'd doze in spite of yourself. You'd be awakened by your partner, or a bunch of rats fighting over a fellow's iron ration who lay out in front and had no further use for them. The routine there, an hour on the firing step, and an hour filling sandbags, and an hour lying down. Lovely! Personally, I got on all the patrols I could wangle. Listening patrol, reconnoitring patrol and bombing patrols. You could sleep down in the dugouts most of the day, and besides you had a chance of getting wounded at night and get back for a while.

The support trenches were damp and full of rats, but still we could get some sleep. We had one week in the firing line, one week in supports, which was working nearly all night bringing stuff in the line, making roads etc.

The weather was wet, the ground soggy for a month or so. We were kept pretty busy. But when we got out for a rest about once a fortnight for two or three days, we got deloused, washed, shaved, clean clothes, the shops, could get wine, beer and champagne to drink. And many a time, in Acheux especially, I remember once about 50 of us in a big estaminet [Estaminet: a French cafe selling wine, beer, and coffee or a cottage with a bar-room] *having a good time. It was well covered with sandbags and, every now and then, between the songs and arguments etc., one could hear the thud of a shell down the street. But most of us were quite relaxed over a bottle and a game of cards, or some fellow rattling up an old "come all ye." We got our strength back again.*

I had my old chum Harold Andrews back with me now. He had been sick and taken off the Peninsula and I missed him till we got together again. He was about 10 years younger than me, but a determined, plucky little devil.

About this time, I got trench fever and was pretty miserable. All you got was medicine and duty. It was pure hell. Stumbling around sick in the cold and wet. I always went on either listening patrols or reconnoitering patrols, and therefore did not do much sentry duty in the line in France.

Listening patrol you went either out in a sap—To explain a sap, it was a straight trench dug out about thirty yards from our line and formed like a T. The end held four or five men with bombs and rifles to be able to put up a fight and give the line time to get ready in case of an enemy attack. On each arm of the T three men could stay in it and watch and report back to the front line without having to get up on top. They were dug out at a distance of from one to two hundred yards of each other and, if we were expecting an attack, there'd be about 12 or 15 men sent out in charge of a Sgt., Corp. or Senior Pvt. and extended about six paces to the right or left of the saps as the case might be. There to lie down and listen.

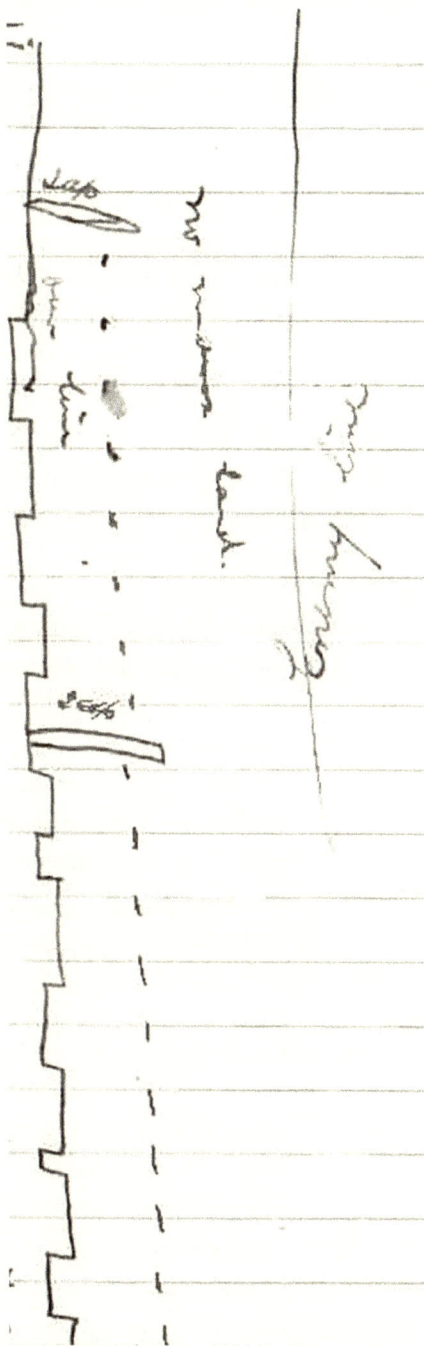

Diagram of the SAP trenches and how men were deployed on listening patrol.

The dots on the diagram would show how the men would file out thru the sap and communication trench and extend to the right. It would then be hard for an enemy spy to get to our line without being seen by one of the patrol at least. If the night was real dark, the patrol would only extend about three paces. I did not like this job, as you'd freeze lying down, and you had such a lot of time to think. Still, I did it for many and many a night.

On bombing patrols we'd go near the German lines and throw a few bombs, and then dropped to the ground and keep still. This was a very nervy job, for as soon as your bombs went off the whole sky was lit with flares and star shells and the shelling of no man's land. All you could do was get into a deep shell hole and stay there and keep perfectly still in whatever position you were in. If you moved at all the star shells or bombs would show you up and you'd had it. A guy, while he was lying out there, could think of a lot of places he'd sooner be. On these patrols you were so keyed up if you kicked a can it sounded like a bell to you. Or if you got tangled in a bit of loose wire or disturbed a bunch of rats feasting on some guy's iron rations you'd be so keyed up you'd think the noise could be heard for miles. Surely a hard time on the nerves. On one patrol, while we were waiting for it to get dark and go over, we were there in the trench standing shoulder to shoulder. Not very pleasant thoughts, because it was pretty certain we were not all coming back. When the officer in charge said "it's time to go, boys" in a low voice, "but cheer up, some of us will never be bothered with rheumatism!" 'Twas a grim joke, but somehow we got a laugh out of it. As it happened we got off lighter than expected; only three wounded, and they were walking cases, so they did not delay our getting back.

Reconnoitering patrol was a party in charge of an officer would go out and crawl along towards the enemy line to see and hear all you could without being seen or heard. If you ran into a German patrol, of course, it was bomb and bayonet to get back to your own lines or, failing that, in some shell hole as quickly as you could. For as soon as anything started in no man's land both sides turned their big guns and machine guns on it and your chance of life was pretty slim. However, we always managed to get back on time.

One foggy night in June, I went out as guide with an English Officer and Sgt. We had to go over to the enemy wire and crawl along by it to see if they had any gaps cut in it, previous to making an attack. It was as black as the inside of a cow and, every time we hooked in a bit of wire or kicked a can or anything, you were so keyed up that you'd think the whole world would hear you. Different times, before we got across no man's land, he told me I was astray, in spite of the star shells and glares falling all around us. This no man's land was about two hundred yards across there, and it seemed a long, long way. Eventually, we got pretty near the wire and we could smell smoke. Just then we heard a voice singing in English. The officer said "I told you so." But I just gripped his arm and whispered to him to listen, and we could hear the Germans talking in a low tone. We followed the wire for what I thought was at least a week (an hour I guess) then we started back. And then the danger was getting in our own line without being shot. For, although the sentry would be warned to look out for our own patrol, that would apply to only a certain distance that you were supposed to go. If you went beyond that and came in to a different part of the line, where the sentries did not know of a patrol, when you hailed the line they would probably shoot first and ask questions afterward. However, we got in the English line and, after a good stiff drink and a few biscuits, the officer sent me back to report, which I did. Then I was dismissed, so I could go down 27 feet underground in the dugout, damp, dirty full of rats and men sleeping in their wet clothes. I'd be asleep in about 2 minutes. Now it takes me hours to go.

The trenches had about a foot of wet mud in them still and the duck boards would float up quite often when it came to rain. 'Twas lovely walking through the trenches, especially if the fellow ahead of you stood on the far end of the duck board and you struck your shin off the far end when it floated up. Our feet and legs got chilled with the cold and wet, and a lot of fellows got trench feet and were sent back. The cold of the water kept the blood from circulating in the feet and legs. We were issued with seal oil to rub our feet and legs to make them watertight. What a stink! Another thing to make us more miserable and uncomfortable, if that were possible.

All this time I was in a kind of haze with trench fever. I cannot remember distinctly what took place lots of times. Just able to do the patrols at night and sleep and do sentry during the day. When in the supports, we would be bringing ammo and rations etc. to the front line, digging sunken roads etc. Some days I was not able to go. So I lay under a sheet of corrugated iron which covered a hole in the side of the trench my buddy and I had dug. He, Harold Andrews, would leave me his water bottle and go off digging. When he came back, I'd have drank his and mine. A half a gallon I guess. That is the way it went on for a week or so. I was reported sick, but no Red Cross man or doctor came near me till, one day, Harold reported me to Lieut. Cliff Rendell, who quickly got me to a field hospital. A good trump he was. He was killed a short time afterwards.

After a few days, I was back in the line again, a little better, back to the usual routine. Our fellows were now mining under the German line, and we had to bring up all the clay in the night in sandbags—a heck of a job. It was wet chalk. We had to bring it along the tunnel, then up 22 steps to the trench, and dump it. Go back again. Where we dumped it in no man's land and it dried and turned white it was called the White City. We had acres of it, and the Germans must have known where it came from, as there was no way to hide it. Certain intervals during the day all work in the tunnel stopped and RE's [Royal Engineers] went in with sound detectors to find if the Germans were mining under us, which they were in some places.

We did a lot of drilling now and training when we went out for a rest; advancing in different formations, word passing, going through a gas chamber with our gas masks on, and drilling with them. After a half hour with your masks on you'd sell your soul for a breath of fresh air. Word passing game gave the officers much trouble, and us much amusement. We were in the open drilling, learning to advance, extended six paces from each other. We'd run so far and lie down, still keep your formation. If the officer passed an order from the right to the left, you'd roll over and pass it to the next man. You can imagine what the order was like after passing it through maybe 200 men! One I still can remember. I was on the left and the officer on the right sent this order: "Open rapid fire at the house on the left; prepare to advance." You can easily understand why the advance was a failure. When the order got over to the left it was "Can you lend me three and four pence, I'm going to a dance." He tried to find out where the twist began but could not pin it down to anyone in particular. That evening we had to listen to a long talk about the seriousness of changing an order. After that they came along pretty near what they were intended to be.

The weather was bad; rain, wet snow, frost, and in the line 'twould break your heart. Standing hour after hour in that cold mud and water. I still kept on night patrol every night I could to keep out of the trench duty at night. For after night patrol you'd get from 6 to 8 hours in the dugout to sleep or rest. They were about 30 feet underground. 'Twas damp and the pump was continually working up top trying to keep the water pumped out and fresh air in, but 'twas safe. You could hear or feel the continuous war of the guns overhead and the pound of bursting shells, but they were muffled by the earth and, once you got asleep, fellows crawling over you with muddy boots did not faze you a bit, you were so used to the misery and dirt. We were more like animals than humans. There were two things that kept us going, hunger—we were always hungry—and the will to live, in spite of it all. Rats gave us a bit of trouble down there too, but they also helped us out in the food line. We'd eat all the biscuits in our emergency ration kit and bring in a badly eaten up kit to prove that the rats ate it. 'Twas said that the rats were a lot fonder of Newfy rations than they were of those of the Regulars. "I wonder why," one officer wanted to know, "the rations are all the same, yet the Newfies have to have theirs renewed every second day."

They gave our front lines an awful dusting with HE [High Energy Explosives] for days. And it kept us busy filling sandbags and building up again. We were withdrawn to the 2nd line and stayed in dugouts there and, a few at a time, did duty in the front line. Next afternoon [April 4, 1917] we were in the dugout and Joe Crane was entertaining us with some "come-all-yes." He was singing Gary's Rocks, a song about a logger called Young Munroe, when a call came for stretcher bearers. A machine gun crew in the front line had got a direct hit. I remember one of the crew, Joe Shaheen, a Maronite, he could speak and read Turkish, he was wounded in the leg and lost it. Joe Crane was killed bringing him out.

We had an Eskimo with us, Johnny Shiwak, he was a sniper and a good one. Dr. Wakefield brought him up from the Labrador. He was very shy and lonely, but I got to be quite friendly with him by talking of seal and duck hunting etc. Once in a while I sneaked out for a few minutes to his sniping post when it was near. We would talk for hours and often he would say "will it ever be over till I get home again." He was a great shot and had a lot of notches on his rifle. He said sniping was like swatching seals. He was killed, so I guess his spirit is back in his beloved Labrador.

Records indicate that Johnny Shiwak was killed on November 20, 1917, at Masnieres. It was not due to a deficiency of his training as a sniper. He almost certainly received training from Hesketh Hesketh-Prichard, the foremost sniper in the British army, for which services Hesketh-Prichard was awarded the MC and DSO. Hesketh-Prichard was brought in to train snipers in the RNR, perhaps at least partially because he had been involved in an expedition of discovery across Labrador and into Québec in 1910 and was familiar with both the country and the people. Johnny Shiwak was killed by a direct hit of an incoming artillery round and no amount of skill or training could have saved him. Prichard wrote several books on his various life experiences, including *Through Trackless Labrador* and *Sniping in France.*

We sometimes had brigade concerts behind the lines when we were in France where Tommy Morrissey's singing of Paddy McGuinty's goat and Darby's Ram were always good for an encore. We did pretty good as regards drinks when we went out for a rest. There was beer a lot better than Egyptian beer, vin blanc and vin rouge and champagne, which was only five francs a bottle, so sometimes we could get to forget our miseries and loosen up our nerves again. I never was much for drinking, but over there I found it good; it relaxed you after being so tense always in the line and on patrols, etc. and I pitied fellows who would not take it.

In France it was different in the trenches, than on the Peninsula. The trenches were farther apart mostly and one never looked over hardly, unless in the night. And one got an overpowering urge to peep out in the daylight and see the ground in front of you and, as they had snipers buried and hidden everywhere out there, many is the fellow lost his life that way.

Our latrines were holes about twelve foot square about 9 ft. deep with rows of boxes with four gallon oil tins in them, placed around as thick as they could stow, and when one wanted a rest from the front line you'd ask the officer could you go to the latrines. They were a kind of community meeting place; you'd get a seat, down pants, light a cigarette, and begin to swap news with those around; news from home, from pals who were gone back wounded, when the next mail was expected, when the next drive was, and so on. It was a great thing for the morale. About twice a day you'd get there if you possibly could.

The mail from home also played a part in keeping the morale up. How we longed for mail when we got it, swapped the news, read the papers etc. and commented on it. A few days were past, then you'd be looking forward for the next one. Then parcels from home containing smokes, chewing tobacco, etc. I got to chew like a goat when one was standing to in the half hour before dawn, and the same before dark. You could not smoke or talk. Everyone just stood shoulder to shoulder with your rifle in your hand. That was the time attacks would generally take place. I hated these times; all one could do was think. Then about evening, after the stand to, you'd get orders as follows: stand down sentries take up their positions; bombing patrols, listening patrols and reconnoitering patrols, move off. And each man would do what he had been detailed for during the day. A weary, dreary, old time no sleep or rest even when one went out in supports for a rest.

Once in the latrines, a young chap called Frayne, who had been only two days in the line, was speaking to me and said he was going to have a look over the top. I told him not to, as a sniper had it set, and a couple of our chaps had been killed here last week. He looked at me in the usual way of the new recruits, like as if I was kidding him, so he stood up and had a look and 'twas his last, for he fell down on top of me with a bullet between his eyes. You couldn't tell them. Another thing they wouldn't believe was when they got issued a day's rations in the morning that it had to do the whole day; they'd eat the most of it for breakfast a few days and then they'd get over that.

We often stayed at Louvencourt, and the people of that village looked after the graves of our dead there. I remember the 27th June, 1916 when we, at least the Catholic members of our regiment, received Holy Communion there. There were over 300 of us in the churchyard there. There were quite a number of graves of young French men from eighteen to twenty-one who were killed in August, 1914, and the women and girls cried right openly in the church. I expect we reminded them of their own *sons and brothers who had been killed. When we marched off to the front line, they lined the streets and waved to us. Only four days after, there were only very few of that bunch left.*

The Battle of Beaumont-Hamel

There is no discernible break in the diary at this point but, as in many instances, there were long periods when time did not allow Howard to continue writing his narrative. In this instance, it was in January of 1950. There would have been no fishing activity underway that would have taken him from his writing. Moreover, by that year he had turned over his business to his son, Bill, who had returned home from his own adventures in the British Army in North Africa and Italy during wwii. However, Howard was plagued with a weak heart and other health conditions he attributed to his time in the trenches, and it was often enough that he was confined to bed for lengthy periods in this time of his life recovering from such a bout. In this case, there is no indication of how long the gap in time was before he resumed his narrative.

About the first of June, we started training for the big drive, and we trained hard.

The weather was still wet and cold. We did a lot of drilling when we were out for a rest; manoeuvres and bombing and so on, between which we got an hour or two in the estaminets and got a few bottles of wine or champagne or beer and forgot about our troubles for a while. At night we brought shells and other gear into the front line. It was hard work and dangerous. One night a bunch of us going in with shells went astray under the fog and went out right under our own big guns. Before we realized where we were, they fired just as we were in front of them and one of my buddies, Paddy Green of Point Verde (Placentia), was made stone deaf. We got back out of it in a hurry. We got back and found we had turned and gone to the rear instead of where the smaller guns were, nearer the front line.

The weather was always wet and cold and we were sure miserable lying and creeping along on the wet ground on patrols and up to your knees in mud in the trenches. I often think of the lines in Robert Service's poem "We'd hunger and thirst and die, but first we'd live, by the God's we'd live!" for it was a great experience to be able to look back at and say "I was there."

About this time, we made a raid on the German lines to take prisoners and get information. Those taking part in it were well fed and drilled for weeks so they knew just what to do. The raid was a success in one way. They killed a lot of men and took the uniforms off them and found out what regiments they belonged to. Fred Neil [Frederick O'Neil] *got the military medal for throwing back a live bomb into the trench. He lost most of his hand, but he saved a lot of our men. One of our chaps, Phillips* [George Gordon Phillips], *jumped into a whole trench full of Germans and all our fellows could hear were screeches and groans from the trench. They had to leave him there, but he turned up next evening all rags and blood and wounds. Seems he must have cleaned the whole trench out of Germans and got out and hid in shell holes until next evening.*

Interestingly, Howard Morry makes no mention of the officer who led these raids, Captain Bertram Butler. Capt. Butler was actually a distant relative of Howard's (third cousin, once removed). There were two raids, one on the 25th of June and the second on the 27th, the first not having succeeded in its objectives. Butler was awarded the Military Cross for his role in leading these important reconnaissance raids. In all likelihood, neither man knew of their relationship to one another.

Before the first of July, one of our chaps, Edmund Edgar [actually Private Edwin Edgar Jr., Regt. # 737], *a buddy of mine, got a cheque for $25.00 on the 28th of June. We had to go to the next village to cash it. But Capt. Rowsell would not give him a pass to go. But he and I, with the help of one of our good Sgts., sneaked off. I went to see the Sarge with Edgar (I won't mention his name)* [almost certainly Joe McKinley, who also helped him out when he needed to get leave for his marriage in Edinburgh] *and said "Sergeant, what would you do for a couple of bottles of champagne?" He knew that the officer had refused Ed permission to go. Well he said "I'd be as blind as the sphinx for two hours." Well that was all we wanted. We cashed the cheque and were back without being missed. Edgar and I went with a couple of bottles of champagne for the Sergeant. He is alive yet, a real man he was, a born leader. He'd get men to follow him to the gates of hell. Edgar divided the money left over in our Platoon. Of course there was lots of champagne and wine for some of us that night, as it was considered unlucky to bring money in the line with you. We had a nice time that night and on the first of July, Edgar was killed. A very likeable chap.*

On the 28th day of June, we came on to the village of Acheux and got outfitted for the drive. Some of us were issued with bombs, more got ladders to throw across the trenches, and we all had a triangular piece of tin to tie to our backs, so as the (our) artillery would see us and not shell us from the air.

On the 29th and thirtieth we knew we were for it. So we all wrote letters home and left messages with our chums if we should be killed. Some of them were sure they were going to be killed, and I know of a couple of chaps who thought that way and were killed. It's strange how some chaps seemed to know they were not coming back from the drive. We knew what we were in for. I'll give you three instances I know. Mike Flynn, a lovely kid from central Newfoundland, wrote about a dozen letters that night, and I asked him what he was writing so many for, and he said these were the last he'd write. He seemed like a damned man. I tried to jolly him along but he could not seem to throw off the depression that was on him. The second, laughing, carefree Jimmy Howard, who said "the bullet that kills one, kills two." Strange to say his mother died after she heard the news of his death. Then there was Joe Penney, from Carbonear. He was engaged to my sister [Beatrice Mary Morry, born September 22, 1888; afterwards married Dr. Louis J. Giovannetti, June 7, 1923], and that evening he came to me with a letter and ring and said "give this to Trixie when you get home." I said "why not keep them, you'll see her as soon as me," but he said "no, I'm not going back." He also was killed. A fine chap. He could have had his discharge, but would not take it.

On the night of the 29th, we left to march in to the line. We left the roads and marched through fields and byroads. We sang songs and talked when marching easy. The songs were "My Little Gray Home in the West," "Take Me Back to Dear Old Blighty," "Down on the Farm," "When You Wore a Tulip" and the favorite one was "When the Great Red Dawn is Shining." Poor chaps; only about one out of twelve were left uninjured or alive after the next day.

On the afternoon of the 30th of June we were all briefed to our part in the next day's advance and knew that zero hour was 7 a.m. Unfortunately, or fortunately, whichever way one looked at it, being married, I was picked among the 10 percent who were kept back about three miles in reserve for bringing up rations as the troops advanced.

The morning of the 1st of July was lovely, once the ground fog cleared away. At dawn, eight of us were sent in with rations, and brought it around to the boys in the trenches. I never felt so low as I did that morning. All the chums were going over and I kept back with some others. Anyway, Victor Carew, my cousin from Cape Broyle, and I stayed in and were there when the boys went over.

But the advance that was scheduled for 7 was postponed till 9 a.m. The officers all synchronized their watches and then began counting—9 minutes to go...8 minutes to go, and so on. Each minute seemed an eternity. Our chaps got up in the reserve trenches. By and by, the officers said "This is it boys, over we go." Then there were only the ration party and very few others left in the line. The very minute they went over the top all hell broke loose. The Germans sure were ready and waiting. When our fellows got up to advance, Jerry opened with everything he had and shelled no man's land, the trenches and supports. There were two big gaps cut in our wire and the Germans must have had every gun trained on them. Most of our chaps were killed before they reached our own front line. You could see nothing but shell bursts and men and sods going up in the air. The machine guns were mowing them down. You could see nothing but dust and flame. You could not hear nor see with the noise of the bursting shells, and the crack of rifle bullets and the dust. After about an hour or less it was over and our front line was blown almost level, also our supports.

Victor Carew and I got together and started out—you could hear the bullets from machine guns swishing by at our feet. We had to be right behind them with the food. But there was no advance. We, with the others, were told to come back, as there was no rations needed. In fact, we both started off after the bunch and went a few yards and when we saw what was doing, we got back to the line again pretty quick. The officers knew that the advance was a failure and that our regiment was wiped out. So we never left the trench, except to go back to Headquarters with messages and feed the very few that got back to the line.

The front line was like a butcher shop in Hell, with our wounded dragging themselves in and falling down in the trench.

We had thought hard of being detailed for the ration party. That day we were sure glad to get back in the line again. The

*first of the ration party to be killed was Quigley from St. John's.
He did not get ten feet. We brought him in at nightfall. Our front
line and Communications trenches and the Reserves were all
smashed level and we made shelter in the deepest part of the
trenches we could find. There were very few places not blown
down. The ground in front was all smoking and all shell holes,
and the groans and cries of the wounded were awful to hear.*

*At noon I was sent in to bring in the 10 percent reserves and
Quartermaster Capt. Summers, but the order was counter-
manded just before I left for it. So I brought in Capt. Summers
and a Quartermaster Sgt., I forgot his name now* [Almost
certainly CQMS C. Allan Cleary, Regt. #679; he was the only
Quartermaster Sergeant to lose his life at Beaumont-Hamel].
*It was nearly evening, and when we came to the supports Jerry
had again started shelling. I told them to keep low and do as I
did, as they were not used to trench warfare. Going up a support trench or communication trench I heard a shell coming
our way and threw myself down flat. It burst over me and
then, as they did not lie down, both were blown to pieces. If
they had lay down, neither one would have been killed. I had
to go report their death to the Colonel. I reported to Colonel
Hadow. He was sorry to hear of their death. They were both
good men.* [Summers is officially listed as dying July 16 of
wounds received on July 1.]

*The shelling was heavy then and it started to rain like hell.
There was not hardly a man to be seen. If the Germans had
advanced, they could have walked through. After a while, I
came across Charlie Parsons, "C" Company Signaller, and
Paddy McDonald, "D" Company Cook. We got together a few
pieces of corrugated roofing and stuck it up to keep the rain
off. We just got in there and had a smoke when BANG came a
shell, followed quickly by three or four more. When we looked
around, our roof was gone but we were unhurt. McDonald was
a very strong broad shouldered chap who had knocked around
quite a bit before he enlisted, same as I did. Never saw him since*

that day, though he got home O.K. He was from Salmonier. We used to have many a yarn when we got a quiet time. What a great gift speech is.

All day long we were watching through glasses and, any of our chaps moved from where they were lying, the Germans would shoot them. The big piece of tin on their backs, that was meant to save life, cost the lives of many of our chaps that day. The least stir, the sun glittered on the tin and gave them away. There wasn't any shell fire, but you could hear the crack of the snipers' rifles all day. The Germans sniping our wounded. They paid dearly for it afterwards.

At nightfall we went out to try and treat some wounded and it was a job. The gaps we had cut in our wire cut for the advance were piled high with dead in all shapes and forms, an awful sight to see. My buddy at this job for the first part of the night was Leo De Lacey, a little fellow from St. John's, but tough and saucy and brave. We brought in three or four, but it was hard to find them. Every shell hole contained a dead or wounded man and

Three who didn't make it. The three soldiers shown above were cousins of Howard Morry who died in battle. Victor and Vincent Carew (left and centre) were brothers from Cape Broyle. Victor died November 20, 1917, preceded by his brother who died on July 10, 1917. L. Cpl. James Carter died the same day and in the same battle as Victor, at Marcoing Copse.

it was a nervy job, crawling into the holes and feeling round to see if they were dead or wounded for, though, during the day we could hear the cries of help from the shell holes, at night there was not a sound, as the poor fellows were afraid to call out, lest the Germans would hear them and kill them. One of them told

M ESSAGE.

From
Lieut.-General SIR AYLMER HUNTER-WESTON K.C.B. D.S.O.
To
All OFFICERS, N.C.O.'s and MEN of the VIII. Army Corps.

In so big a command as an Army Corps of four Divisions (about eighty thousand men) it is impossible for me to come round all front line trenches and all billets to see every man as I wish to do. You must take the will for the deed, and accept this printed message in place of the spoken word.

It is difficult for me to express my admiration for the splendid courage, determination and discipline displayed by every Officer, N.C.O. and Man of the Battalions that took part in the great attack on the BEAUMONT-HAMEL-SERRE position on the 1st July. All observers agree in stating that the various waves of men issued from their trenches and moved forward at the appointed time in perfect order, undismayed by the heavy artillery fire and deadly machine gun fire There were no cowards nor waverers, and not a man fell out. It was a magnificent display of disciplined courage worthy of the best traditions of the British race.

Very few are left of my old comrades the original "Contemptibles," but their successors in the 4th Division have shewn that they are worthy to bear the honours gained by the 4th Division at their first great fight at Fontaine-au-Pire and Ligny, during the great Retreat and greater Advance across the Marne and Aisne, and in all the hard fighting at Ploegsteert and at Ypres.

Though but few of my old comrades, heroes of the historic landing at Cape Helles, are still with us, the 29th Division of to-day has shown itself capable of maintaining its high traditions, and has proved itself worthy of its hard earned title of "The Incomparable 29th."

The 31st New Army Division, and the 48th Territorial Division, by the heroism and discipline of the units engaged in this their first big battle, have proved themselves worthy to fight by the side of such magnificent regular Divisions as the 4th and 29th. There can be no higher praise.

We had the most difficult part of the line to attack. The Germans had fortified it with skill and immense labour for many months, they had kept their best troops here, and had assembled North, East, and South-East of it a formidable collection of artillery and many machine guns.

By your splendid attack you held these enemy forces here in the North and so enabled our friends in the South, both British and French, to achieve the brilliant success that they have. Therefore, though we did not do all we hoped to do you have more than pulled your weight, and you and our even more glorious comrades who have preceded us across the Great Divide have nobly done your Duty.

We have got to stick it out and go on hammering. Next time we attack, if it please God, we will not only pull our weight but will pull off a big thing. With such troops as you, who are determined to stick it out and do your duty, we are certain of winning through to a glorious victory.

I salute each Officer, N.C.O. and Man of the 4th, 29th, 31st, and 48th Divisions as a comrade-in-arms and I rejoice to have the privilege of commanding such a band of heroes as the VIII. Corps have proved themselves to be.

H.Q., VIII. CORPS,   AYLMER HUNTER-WESTON,
    4th July, 1916.   *Lieut.-General.*

ARMY PRINTING AND STATIONERY SERVICES A. 7/16 80,000.

Our Regt was in the 29 division. in Jullipoli France & Belgium. Only 64 answered roll call

on July 1st 1916. out of over then eight hundred men

Propaganda message following the defeat at the Somme. This message was distributed to all men under the British Command after the stunning defeat of July 1. Propaganda in wartime is normal, but perhaps in this instance it was done in the vain hope that calling a defeat a victory would somehow soften the blow to those who had suffered most.

us that as soon as it got dark the Germans came out and bayoneted any wounded they saw. Charlie Parsons and I brought in a lot of wounded later in the night. The bravest and luckiest man I knew; got an MM and Bar and came home without a scratch. It was awful, the dead and dying, the burst of shells and then the star shells lighting up everything as bright as day. One could only make a few yards at a time when a flare or star shell would burst. Then you would have to stay still. If you moved at all you'd be spotted. I never thought the human mind could stand so much.

Some chaps who were wounded struggled to get back to our lines. Some of them made a good job of bandaging their wounds and stopping the bleeding and others just lay there and let themselves bleed to death. A few badly wounded, or with painful wounds, just cut an artery and died. Guess when they were not rescued the first night they could not take it, the poor fellows.

We brought in a young fellow the second night who had not a mark on him except a bullet graze across his nose but he was stone blind. He thought it was still night. It must have been awful long to him.

After the wounded, we began to bring in the dead. We took 89 dead out of one gap in the barbed wire and 72 out of the

A page from Howard Morry's paybook. This paybook page shows the transfer of command of Howard Morry's Company from Captain Rowsell to Captain Donnelly after the 1st of July. Rowsell was seriously injured at Beaumont-Hamel and, though he recuperated and returned to the Regiment later, both he and Donnelly were victims of the war. Donnelly had signed Howard Morry's attestation papers on December 17, 1914.

other, it was an awful sight for us survivors to see our good friends and buddies for years, piled up like that. But we were pretty exhausted and stunned by what had happened to us and we were called in and told to go down in the dugouts and get some sleep. If the Germans had to try and advance that night they could have gone right through as the 29th Division lines were held by a very few exhausted men.

Only 68, to be exact, answered roll call the first evening, and the ration parties were counted in with them. Sixteen in our C Company. Neither officer and only one non-com. Me being senior private, I was heading patrols and doing sergeant's work for a couple of weeks. I would not take stripes. Too much trouble. Some of the older chaps wanted me to, and the officers too. They said I'd be sorry when the new bunch came and I had to take orders from the new NCOs just from home and they'd have their own friends and would give the old fellows the dirty end of the stick. I was just about taking them when I got sick. Captain Donnelly and Rowsell both told me many times that I'd be a

Captain James Donnelly (left) and Reginald S. Rowsell (right, bottom right).

142 WHEN THE GREAT RED DAWN IS SHINING

sergeant in a month, they'd see to it. Time I got out of the hospi-
tal, both these men were dead.

What an awful waste of human life ("war is Hell" is surely
true). It leaves behind it a trail of broken men, broken hearts
and lives and broken and unhappy homes.

Aftermath of the Battle:
Reforming the Regiment,
and on to Ypres

*F*or six days we moved back in the day, and moved back in
in the night, searching for wounded and bringing in some
dead. There were only 69 of us left in the Battalion. About the
third day, we got a draft of about twenty new hands and Martin
Kent and I were sent to bring them in. Poor devils, never under
fire before, and when we got them to the trenches and they saw
the dead lying around, they got scared, some of them very badly.
They were hard to manage and the only way we could do it was
Martin lead and I brought up the rear. They would not listen to
us when we told them to lie down etc., as we were only Privates,
so the result was we had seven of the thirteen, four killed and
three wounded going in. The other six lived to be old soldiers. It's
strange but the new drafts came and went, but the old sweats
still remained. The new hands were killed or wounded before
they had time to learn how to survive.

Well after the first of July, about the sixth I think, we got a couple of small drafts and we left for a rest, and what a night march
that was, all our chums gone, and we were strangers. We were just
dragging along the road, when Sgt. Major Dicks went in about 10
p.m. and bought a couple of accordions and put one in front and

one in the rear and they started up the "Banks of Newfoundland,"
and we cheered right up. Only 16 in our company of over 200 who
had marched in singing a few days before remained.

So we marched till 12 p.m., then we lay down by the road-
side and slept till dawn, when we marched again till next eve-
ning when we came to a place called Abbeville where we started
to form a new Nfld. Regt. on the survivors of the old.

The official war diary of the RNR records that they left the
trenches on July 6, 1916, as Howard records. But there is some
confusion between his account of where they were billeted. In the
official record it is stated that, for the first few days (July 6-7) of
rest, the troops were billeted at Englebelmer, and then they moved
a short distance to better shelter at Mailly-Maillet (misspelled
Maillet-Mailly in the war diary) from July 8-14. The reason for the
move was the heavy bombardment of Englebelmer while they were
there, which claimed the life of Lieut. Owen Steele and possibly
other soldiers not mentioned in the record. This makes more sense,
as both of these small villages are close to the battlefield, within a
day's march, whereas Abbeville would have been too far away for a
march of a day or two.

When we had rested for five days, we went in and took over
our old lines again, and our first job was to finish burying our
dead. And some job that was to take those blackened, swollen
bodies, take the equipment off them. When the equipment belt
was opened, what a rush of air out of the swollen bodies! Then
we had to take their pay books, letters, watches etc., mark them,
and turn them in, so that they could be sent to their relatives.
We had to wear gas masks, and just dug a hole 'longside the
body and rolled them in with a simple prayer.

It's a grand thing that mothers could not see the way their
sons died.

One lovely Sunday afternoon [July 16, 1916], we were sitting
in our bay in the trench. Paul Drucken was looking out through

the periscope. Leo De Lacey, Harry Mifflin, Harold Andrews, Willis White, Lewis Head and I were enjoying the sun and fanning off when Lieut. Grant came along to pick out a bunch for listening patrols and reconnoitring patrols for the night. Abe Myers ("Pigshit," he was always called, I never knew his real name until I read it in the casualty list) he was a nice chap, but as I was saying he was coming along the trench with a message for the lieutenant, when the lieutenant asked if he was a good man. De Lacey said "I don't know how good he is, but I know he is the devil to jump." He was about ten steps down the dugout in a second, he had heard the shell coming before any of us. The lieutenant took a few steps to see where Myers had gone when the shell burst and a piece hit Lieut. Grant. He lived long enough to tell Mifflin who to write to and he took off his ring and told him where to send that, and he said "there are a few pounds in my pocketbook, take it and drink to my memory when you go out." He was a grand young fellow and only lived a few minutes.

About an hour after that, we were all sitting on the firestep eating our evening meal, when a big shell hit and burst about ten or fifteen yards in front of our trench and blew the body of a sergeant of the Monmouth in on top of us. We had buried him there about a week before that. He was too decayed to remove when we found him. We were all covered with scraps of human flesh and every one of us began to vomit and kept at it the whole night, in fact until we got new uniforms, as we could smell it for days afterwards. We had to get on our gas masks to re-inter him. We buried him in the shell hole.

We stayed a week in the line this time, and then we moved out to Louvencourt where we were in billets again. We got a night's sleep, a wash and a shave, clean clothes and, best of all, we went to a de-lousing plant. We went to Abbeville to be deloused. We were nearly all skinned from scratching, and the thought of a bath and clean clothes was something to look forward to. I remember well the first time we went there. We were *marched to the plant, about 50 men at a time and marched into the yard, where we stopped, stripped, took off our boots, and put the rest of our clothes in a bundle, and they were put through some furnace or oven and, when we got them back, it took us hours to get our own. Then we were all crowded into a room as thick as we could stow. The floor above was all holes and water sprayed down over us for a minute or two. We were supposed to wash ourselves. There was an inch or two of muddy water on the floor. You might call it mud, after all the dirt and lice that had collected on us for months was washed into it. After a few minutes more we were herded out in the open to dry ourselves, and a new bunch went in. In the meantime, here were hundreds of men parading around naked. The girls in the plant spent more time at the windows than they did at our clothes. It's not often a gal gets to see 100 naked men standing in a line. Some of us were shy and some were not. I guess some of the girls were uneasy for a while. I remember seeing our fellows going around for hours trying to get their clothes. We put them in one bundle, but anyone who had not his clothes marked was out of luck, as they must have mixed them up deliberately so they could watch the fun. Personally I got my own tunic but a trousers that could not fit a boy of twelve. Eventually, we got straightened out and were marched off to our billets feeling quite fresh again. But that feeling did not last long unless you had blue ointment to rub on your hairy parts to kill the lice as fast as the eggs come to life.*

There is, once again, a discrepancy between the official war diary and Howard's account of where the remnants of the RNR spent their time during this period. While he refers to their billets as being at Louvencourt, the official record places them at Acheux, initially, and then Beauval for the majority of the time. These villages were all close to one another, and it is entirely possible that the troops referred to the area where they stayed by the name of the largest amongst the local villages. In fact, it is possible they were ignorant of their precise location, since none of them would have had maps. The passages that follow record events that occurred during this time that were impressed on Howard's mind and memory. It is interesting that he made no mention whatsoever of the fact that, during this period, the RNR was visited on several occasions and inspected by various "dignitaries" from Newfoundland, including Prime Minister Sir Edward Morris. This is emblematic of his disdain for authority of any form, but particularly for those who put the lives of ordinary Newfoundlanders at risk while sitting out the war at home themselves. It's impossible to say how much Howard's sentiments were held in common by his fellow soldiers but he most likely represented a fair number of them in this regard. No doubt the "dignitaries" believed their presence gave a great uplift to the men; if only they knew the truth.

Leo De Lacey, Howard Morry, and Jack Davis after the battle of Beaumont-Hamel. Howard's inscription on the back, written years later to his daughter Elsie, reads, "Beauval, July 23, '16. Lost my cap in the July Drive. Never got one for months & lucky I got the Australian. Jack Davis lost his too & was stuck with a steel helmet for a long while. The other chap Leo De Lacey of St. John's. Keep this one for your album gal. Thin, and a queer look in my eyes. Only 67 of us answered the Roll Call July 1, 1916 out of 890 that went over. What a day, what a memory. But we beat the Charge of the Light Brigade for Bravery & brought honour to ourselves and our country. No. 726, Howard Morry."

We were at Louvencourt this time the mail came and we had letters from home. The mail was always looked forward to eagerly, and read over and over, and talked about, and then you'd wonder if you'd still be alive when the next mail came. Also we got to write a few lines home. We were not allowed to tell anything, just "I am well" and a few personal things.

We got reinforcements and started to build the Regt. up again on the skeleton of the old Regt. We old fellows were told to set a good example to the kids coming out. There I was promoted to Corporal, but I did not want the bother of stripes, as it tied one down too much, so I went away without leave for a couple of days with some Aussies, and got rid of them quite easy. I was glad to be free again and kept clear of them after. But I was sorry for it afterwards when we old sweats were ordered around by kids but a few months formed up. I guess if I'd remained longer, I'd have taken them again, as I had just as much on my mind as Senior Private as I would if I were a Sgt.

On the 24th of July, we were again at Abbeville for a rest. We were billeted amongst Aussies whilst in Abbeville, and there were seven of us and five Aussies in one estaminet. Jacky Davis and De Lacey were amongst us. I forget the other three names. My stomach was upset; I felt sick to my stomach all the time. Could imagine I smelled the dead off my hands each time I went to eat. Guess handling so many of them got on my nerves. Started to write a letter home and when I went to date it I said

The Second Newfoundland Regiment forming in St. John's, Summer of 1916. These were recruits who filled the ranks after the devastation at Beaumont-Hamel.

"gosh, this is my birthday." One of the Aussies heard me and said we must celebrate. He said "I got 50 quid from home yesterday and that's a good way to spend it," so he went off and got a dozen bottles of Champagne for a start. I don't know how many more after that, as we spent the day singing and telling stories etc.

About 2 in the afternoon we heard yells and swearing from an orchard up on the hill back of us. By and by we heard "Newfoundland, Newfoundland!," and I knew our fellows were in a row again and wanted help, and I said "come on boys, let's go," and out we went and up over the hill. I just had a nice happy jag and, as I was going up the hill, a big Tommy sergeant ran down to meet me. It didn't seem to me that we were fighting. I was feeling at peace with the whole world. He gave me a wallop in the face and, before I knew it, I was lying back of the estaminet and one of the Australians giving me hell for letting a Tommy knock me out. What a scrap that was. Seems some of our fellows were eating fruit in the orchard and the English soldiers tried to stop them because, whatever damage was done by the Regiment, the Division or Brigade had to pay for it. Generally 'twas our fellows to blame. They were a wild mob anyway and it really was too bad, for the most of the British soldiers had only 10 cents a day to spend and we had $1.10 at this time. The brigade was assessed £200 for the orchard and it seems there were two horses bayoneted as well. We did not mind our share of it, but the rest of the Brigade must have felt it bad.

That is the chief reason they disliked us so much. And besides, we laughed at them for saluting their officers at every turn and twist, and being scared of their NCOS. We saluted when we could not help doing otherwise, and did not bother too much about our NCOS, only doing what they wanted us to do, and lots of times covering up for them to keep them from being demoted and coming out of the trenches.

The Aussies went in the line that night and got an awful doing up. I expect Fagan was killed, as he promised to write me and gave me his address, but I never heard from him.

This time we had a big long march and came to Louvencourt again. I remember we had not marched four miles when four of the new draft fell out. Captain Rowsell went back and read the riot act to them. He said "nobody in the Newfoundland Regiment fell out on a route march. That's our record in this 88th brigade. Let us keep it that way." He said "look around you and see what some of the chaps who have had years of it are doing and feel ashamed of yourselves." Some of the fellows were marching in their bare feet with their boots hung over their shoulders. Their feet were either too sore or too swollen with trench foot to wear boots. Our fellows, mostly kids, were just great. They had a record to keep up and they kept it.

On that march, one of my old buddies returned to us after being wounded on the 1st of July (Mark Guy). A ruddy faced, blue-eyed, happy kid, and he sure had grit. He had two bullet wounds in the left breast just above the heart. They went right through him, and here he was, after just three weeks he was back with us again. That is one of the things that a shortage of reserves did. Lots of guys that are dead should be still alive. For want of reinforcements, they were sent back before they had sufficiently recovered from their wounds.

After a half hour or so marching, I noticed him bumping off me now and then as we were marching. He was in the same four I was in. I said to him "are you tired Mark?" The perspiration was rolling off him in a river, and you could see he was out on his feet, but pure determination and grit kept him going. We had a rest of five or ten minutes every hour. The first rest we took, Mark opened his collars and showed us the wounds. They were red and chafed from his pack strap. I wanted him to let me tell the Captain, but he would not let me. He said "No by G-d, they sent me back fit and I'm not going to give in," and we fell in again, and after about a quarter of an hour he just could walk. I took his rifle and Jack Davis from Bell Island took his pack. When Capt. Rowsell on horseback fell back to see how we were marching in his "C" Company, the first thing he saw

the two rifles on my shoulder. He said "what are you doing with
two rifles?" I said "Mark Guy is sick and could not carry it," so
he made him fall out and put him in one of the wagons. When
we went to see him next morning he was marked for hospital
and looked pretty sick, but he smiled and shook hands with us
and wished us luck, and that was the last of Mark. He died
a short while after of lung trouble I believe. Another good kid
gone. [Records do not list a date of death—perhaps he died
after returning home.]

After a while in Abbeville, we marched to Ypres in Belgium.
Six days' march, 150 miles, without losing a man. When we
came to Ypres, before we came to the reviewing stand, our band
struck up The Banks of Newfoundland, and we marched in
with our heads in the air, swinging along like if we just came
on parade, instead of coming right out of the trenches on the
Somme, and marching 150 miles non-stop to Belgium. General
Cayley complimented us and again called us his boys. He
held us in high regard. I believe it was one of the longest forced
marches in the history of the British Army.

This is a very strange departure from the war diary. The official
record shows that the RNR departed ("entrained") at Candas on July
27 and arrived ("detrained") at Hopoutre military railway halt near
Poperinghe, the marshalling point for Ypres, on July 28, where they
remained until July 30. At that time, they were to have proceeded
the remaining short distance to Ypres by train. There is no record
whatsoever of this forced march mentioned by Howard Morry. Did
it ever happen? Was it a false memory brought on by his almost
incessant bouts of trench fever and rheumatic fever during this
period of writing? Was the war diary, written by Lt. Col. Hadow,
written without full possession or admission of the facts? On several
occasions Hadow was noted to have been away for lengthy periods,
possibly due to illness/stress. The subject requires further research
since, as Howard notes, this would have been "one of the longest
forced marches in the history of the British Army" and, if it actually

did occur, the historical record should be changed to reflect this remarkable achievement. Frank Gogos, a Newfoundland author who has conducted extensive research on the RNR, and Graham Skanes, Chair of the Museum Committee of the RNR Museum in St. John's, both point out flaws in Howard's retelling of the events, including the fact that the RNR Band was never in France or Belgium at this time, and that there is no record of this forced march in any other history of the regiment. But a recent discovery lends some credence to Howard's version of the move. There is an oral recording made by Lieutenant John Percy Copp, a Platoon Commander in B Company of the 46th Battalion of the Canadian Expeditionary Force. In this brief recording, he describes a forced march from France to Ypres by his troops shortly after their arrival from Britain on August 10, 1916, which sounds remarkably like that described by Howard Morry, so such troop movements were not unheard of at that time and in that theatre of war.

When I got there I got another attack of Trench Fever that was brought on by lice, of which each of us must have carried at least a million around with us. We were billeted in the basement of what was once a university there and were shelled every day. There were about two feet of water on the floor of our billet. It was all iron beds we had and, in the night, when they were all out on digging parties etc., I was left alone there for hours, and I begged all the fellows to leave candles with me, which they did. And only for that I'd have ended in the nut house. For, as soon as they would all move out, dozens of rats started swimming around from bunk to bunk, and many is the time I knocked them off me. I was scared to sleep and kept the candles going till the boys came home.

One night I must have dozed off for a little while. Suddenly I woke and thought I heard a whispering, and I listened and sure enough there was someone there. It was a poor fellow John Oliver by name, who I had often befriended when fellows were tormenting him. He said "don't be afraid, you'll be alright. I stole away to come back and pray for you." Poor kid, he was a simple poor soul, not looked after too well I expect. He risked severe punishment by coming out of the line without permission. He must have had a wonderful faith in prayer that kid. He hung his beads on the head of my

German Held   German Held

British Held

Ypres Salient

Howard Morry's depiction of the Ypres Salient, redrawn by the author from a diagram in the original diaries of Howard Leopold Morry.

cot and said "the rats won't hurt you" and then he left.

I had to send him away lest he got in trouble for leaving the line.

Belgium was a hard place on me. We were in the Ypres Salient, a wedge driven out in the German line for four or five miles. It would be about a mile or so across the widest part and it was a pure death trap, though we held it at a great cost for sentiment sake, as the big guys did not want any more of Belgium to fall into German hands. They say the British lost 350 thousand men holding this place, and I quite believe it from what I saw while we were there.

With the star shells and flares going up from each line, and the shell bursts as well all over no man's land, made it a pretty lively looking triangle.

We could only dig down two feet when the water came, so we had to fill sand bags and build up. The trenches were shell holes linked up, and the damp and the cold, the lice and the mud, would almost drive you nuts. Especially evenings when that white fog would roll in from the North Sea, and we always had to be in the "qui vive" to see that Jerry did not get some gas over on us with it. It was awful chill and damp till late in morning, when the sun ate up the fog.

I was only a week or so in the front line, when I got taken with rheumatic fever. When I woke there were two Red Cross fellows with a stretcher to take me up top [August 10, 1916]. 'Twas just before day, and 'twas cold and foggy and dark, and I was a sick man and didn't give a damn if I lived or died. I'd had it. They laid me beside a few more guys on stretchers, put our gas masks on, and left us waiting there till the ambulance came to take us away. You folks who never had a gas mask on, especially the first issue ones we had, have no idea how uncomfortable one could be. They were just a small bag of heavy material with chemicals in it to neutralize the gas. There were glasses to see through, but when the masks were buttoned under the neck of your tunic, the only air you got was sucked in through the cloth in the bag. There was a small tube with rubber on the end of it to breath out through, but nothing to breathe in through. Tough, but was better than being gassed.

You can imagine how I felt lying there on the stretcher on the ground with rheumatic fever, gas shells bursting all around, and not able to help yourself. I never felt so helpless in all my life. Guess some would pray. I never was much good at that, though I always admired men who could and did. The only real prayers I said was in the trenches. As a kid my mother taught me "Now I lay me down to sleep" etc., but it was kind of long ago. But after seeing fellows getting toted out now and then, killed in their sleep when it came with shells and guns going full blast, I'd make the sign of the cross, say "God protect me, keep me safe and forgive me my sins," not much to say, but from the heart. Guess it's not so much what you say as much as the way you say and feel about it.

I was moved out to Poperinghe to an emergency hospital that was in one half of a school and convent. There were over three hundred little kids there from two to four years old with tags on them. The sisters had a list of them: where and when they were found, and the clothes they wore and any little words they spoke, so they might be able to find their parents when peace came. It was a sorrowful sight. There was only one Newfy there with me, a chap called Burton from St. John's [likely Private Brendan Burton, Regt. # 2033].

We were treated good there. After staying there a few weeks, I was sent to the third Canadian General Hospital. at Bologne

[August 17, 1916] *where, after a week or so, I began to feel quite well and asked the Doctor, Bruce was his name, to let me up. Which he did for a few hours a day. So next day I got up in the afternoon, and the next day I got up in the morning. The doctor came along and said "I'll have to mark you for duty again." I said "that's O.K. sir, I'm feeling fine." So I was next day detailed cookhouse orderly helping the Sisters dry the dishes etc., and we were having great fun pitching them to one another. Suddenly I woke up in bed again, a Blighty (England) pinned on my pyjamas. So I was bound for old England, and I was delighted!*

Blighty and the Return Home

D ad Morry's story resumes with his account of being transported with other wounded and sick soldiers back to England for treatment. It is clear from his account of the passage of time above that, when these events occurred, he was suffering badly from fever and not in possession of all of his mental faculties, leading to an inability to recall time, dates, and chronology later in life when he wrote his memoirs. Whereas his recollection of these events covers several weeks, in point of fact his military records show that from the time he was evacuated to the first field hospital on August 10 until he was admitted to Wandsworth Hospital outside of London on August 25 covered a period of just over two weeks.

Strangely, one of the most interesting accounts of his time at Wandsworth Hospital is missing in his memoirs and only came down to us through his oral history of those times.

One day, while on the mend, he got talking to another soldier in a bed next to his and discovered that the soldier's name was Bradshaw and that he was from British Columbia. To their surprise and obvious excitement they discovered they were actually related to one another, the Bradshaw family having been connected to the

Windsors of Aquaforte (e.g., Mont and Stan Windsor, Howard's cousins). William George Bradshaw, a Newfoundlander from Placentia, had married Sarah Payne Windsor from Aquaforte, and they had moved to BC where most of their children were born. But their son, William George Jr., had been born in Placentia before they left Newfoundland. Despite this, Bradshaw chose not to join the RNR but instead enlisted in the Canadian Expeditionary Force on March 11, 1915, in Victoria, BC. It was just an amazing coincidence that he should have wound up convalescing at Wandsworth with Howard Morry, his second cousin, once removed.

The commotion they caused by this discovery and the mention of the name Windsor and the place Aquaforte caught the ears of another patient on the ward. He introduced himself as Clifford Ford Windsor and informed them that he too was descended from the Windsors of Aquaforte. He was the son of Peter Ford Windsor, who had left Aquaforte to find his fortune in gold and diamonds in South Africa. In fact, the town where they lived was renamed Windsorton from Hebron, by Cecil Rhodes, in their honour. Clifford Windsor was a survivor of the Battle of Delville Wood, South Africa's equivalent to what Beaumont-Hamel was to the Newfoundlanders or Gallipoli was to the ANZACs. The South African First Infantry Brigade suffered losses of 80% in this, their first major engagement on the Western Front. Compare this to losses by other allied units in the same theatre of war which were closer to 30%. Despite these devastating losses, the South Africans somehow managed to hold onto the Wood as ordered. Clifford recovered from his wounds and went back to the front, but was captured by the Germans and spent the rest of the war as a POW.

Considering what a bewildering coincidence this was, it is amazing that it was not recorded in any one of Dad Morry's WWI memoirs.

Next day I, with hundreds of others, were put on a Red Cross boat for England. All the stretcher cases were kept on deck, afraid the ship would be torpedoed or mined, as quite a few had been lately. The ones that could help themselves were below decks. At that time, the Germans were sinking Red Cross boats whenever they got a chance.

We arrived in Dover on a lovely morning and we were laid out on stretchers on the wharf and, though I was sick, I laughed to myself, as the stretcher bearers would pass by the big looking fellow and take the small ones. It reminded me of fellows barrowing fish at home. I lay there as well as an Aussie called Foster, who was about my size, as we were passed by, and we could hear them say, "these two big b......ds" as they took the smaller ones. And Foster made some pretty queer remarks about the orderlies. I fell asleep and after a while was awakened by the dropping of an empty stretcher on the wharf beside me. The sudden noise almost scared me to death. They put Foster and I on an ambulance. As soon as we got outside the gates, there were women and girls pitching roses in the ambulances as they passed. It was good to see the lovely English faces again, after years of only seeing men, and mud, and sand, etc.

Howard Morry's Aunt "Fanny" (right). Emily Frances Victoria Morry (Fanny) led a group of VAD Nurses overseas at the age of fifty, and almost certainly was at Wandsworth at some point, though perhaps not at the time Howard Morry was there, since she is not mentioned in his narrative.

I was sent to the Third General Hospital, Wandsworth, where I spent two months in bed with rheumatic. I was now quite helpless with rheumatism, but felt real happy when they put me in that nice clean bed and at once fell asleep. When I awoke and looked at the nice clean sheets, the windows and walls, I realized I was under a roof again. It was a wonderful feeling. Every day now I was put in an electric oven. The heat was something awful. This went on for weeks. The ladies from London came and visited us, sat and talked with us, brought candy, flowers and smokes, etc. After a while they changed me from the oven to a hot mud bath, and after a few days I began to feel better. After each bath, the orderlies walked me around, first for a few minutes, and then for a half hour at each time after each bath. I gained every day, and then, after a while, I got along on crutches and finally with a cane.

Finally a lady, Mrs. Moffrey would come almost every afternoon, and took my arm and walked me around the grounds. What great charitable folks they were. I wrote Mrs. Moffrey quite a few times after I left. I was about a month home when her husband wrote me she had died. Guess she wore herself out tending on soldiers and sick in the hospital.

Furlough from Wandsworth Hospital, October 16, 1916.

At length, I was discharged and sent to a convalescent home at Esher, Surrey. It was grand there. We got the best of food, and out in the sun every day. I began to gain strength rapidly, but suffered a lot with a numb kind of feeling in my head. The nurses were all titled ladies of the VAD detachment and were great. Came a day when a chap, Conway, and I were sent off to Wandsworth for a few days under observation, and then before a board of doctors. Then we were brought to 59 Victoria Street, got our back pay and a ten day pass and then to report to the Regt. Headquarters at Ayr.

I stayed a few days in London and then went to our "Home Town," Edinburgh, where the people made me so much at home, and treated us so kindly that we of the First Battalion will never forget and, to this day, when we old vets meet and have a yarn, it's not long before Edinburgh was brought into the conversation.

When I got to Edinburgh, Nellie and her father (sister-in-law and father-in-law) came to meet me, but I missed them and got home before them, and hid behind the door to grab Nellie when she came in. It was good to be back again, but I missed Fredris, as she had been home in Ferryland for over two years.

I reported at the base at Ayr when my leave was up, but spent one last night in a village near Ayr, where a bunch of

James and Nellie Minty, Fredris Minty Morry's father and sister.

ammunition factory girls took me to a dance there. And I had a very nice night there, and I met some of our boys from the depot at Ayr. I say they took me off the train, well they did. They asked me to come with them, but I said I was sorry, but I had to report. But they said you've been having a hard time

(THIRD CLASS)

Identification Card for Government Officer at Port of Arrival in Canada

Name of Passenger ....

Name of Ship **Scandinavian.** Sailing from **Liverpool.**

Date of sailing ......**28-10-16.**..... Country of last permanent residence........................

Name appears on Manifest, page.. line........

| Medical Examination Stamp. | Civil Examination Stamp. | Inland Exchange Order Reads over ....Ry. |

VACCINATION PROTECTED

....

Ship Surgeon's Signature. (SEE BACK)

Allan Liner S. S. "Scandinavian".

(TOP) *The ticket home. Identification card from the scrapbook of Howard Leopold Morry.* (BOTTOM) *A postcard of the* SS Scandinavian *which carried Howard Morry home.*

at the front so we want to show you a good time. They took my equipment off the rack and my kit bag, so of course I had to follow it, and it was sure worth it. Great kids these warm-hearted Scottish lads and lassies.

Spent ten days at Ayr, was examined by a board of doctors again, and marked for home. After another week, got orders and a train ticket to Liverpool, where there were 14 others for home. I forget most of them, but Mike Downey, Andy Coady, Tucker of Portugal Cove were three of them. We were in charge of Sergeant Steele. Was I glad? You tell me!!!! Boy oh Boy! Home, after almost three years of hell.

We had a nice trip home and landed at Quebec, and came from that home by train. Got home at last, still pretty miserable but glad to be home. Fredris looked lovelier than ever, and Phyl was a nice little kid. Being the first from Ferryland home from the war, I was given quite a reception. Guns firing, and flags flying, etc.

Now and again I think of things that were said or happened.

One of my buddies from Ferryland, Jack Barnable, who was wounded at Monchy, had his foot blown nearly off, just above the ankle. He was crawling back with a bunch of our wounded, and he fell behind owing to his foot dragging and getting caught in everything. They were all headed for an old barn, and he told them to go on, he would join them later. When they were gone, he just sat up and cut off his foot with his pocket knife, and that delay saved his life, as the barn where all his comrades were, got a direct hit, and they were all killed.

Another chap, Coombes I think his name was, from Lower Island Cove, got a bullet through both thighs and crawled into a deep shell hole and could not get out. We were passing him by day after day not seeing him down there. It came to rain on the seventh day, and he floated and scrambled up on the top, where we found him and brought him in. He had lived for days on the emergency rations of his dead comrades who had crawled in the shell hole with him and died.

There are a couple of instances of the grit and endurance of our boys. Dan Moore lost a leg. I met him a few years after the war. I asked him how he was. "Fine," says Dan. "But I will never be able to kick my own ass again!" He always said he'd like to die like a man with his boots on.

Well the war was a great experience. Now I often sit and think and go back to these days. And, in my mind's eye, I can see those that never came back like they were in life, laughing boys full of fun and devilment. And then, when I look at my buddies that did come back, I often wonder who had the best of it. Those that didn't come home or those that did.

After a couple of months home, I got orders to report to Headquarters in St. John's. I thought I was to go back again, and went around and said goodbye to everyone, but when I went to the office I found I was for "discharged—unfit for further service."

I got a telegram from home saying to come at once as Fredris was dangerously ill. So, after being discharged, I left immediately for home and found Fredris in a raging fever. She had contracted scarlet fever and was dangerously ill for weeks. Eventually she got over it, but had sinus trouble after it, and spent months in the hospital afterwards, and had gotten all her frontal bones on one side of her head taken away. She had wonderful spirit and pluck.

After the winter was over, we went to live by ourselves in an old house, but we were happy as could be, and I began to clear away to build a house on the site of what was our old house. It was an old stone house, the oldest on this side of the Atlantic, and it took me weeks to level off the ruins before I could begin to build mine. I got lots of help from all the neighbours at building it, and there is not a door or window in it but is a memory of an old friend and neighbour, many of whom have passed to their reward, may God be good to them. Now it's everyone for himself and the Devil take the hindmost. We are developing a different breed of Newfoundlanders, as time goes on and we are having more connection with the outside world. People are getting wiser to many things, live better and dress better than our forefathers, but miss the happy, contented, neighbourly style of long ago. But, however, the ordinary Newfoundlander, in the outports anyway, is still a good trump and always willing to lend a helping hand to a neighbour or friend.

My first year home I fished with Jim Barnable, who took me, though I was not very well able to work, for which I always thought a lot of him. We made $1120 a man, as fish was twelve dollars a quintal, and things were very reasonable. I bought lumber to build my house and then, that Fall, we got a gratuity from the Government of about $100 a year for each year served overseas, which helped a lot. At first I was paid off a sick man I got $15 to buy a Civvy suit; the price of any kind of a half decent ready-made was $65. So that was the way the first discharged men of the Royal Newfoundland Regt. were treated.

A delegation of us went to see the Premier, Sir Richard Squires, to get a deal on the lines of the Canadian Pensions, but were told that we got what we signed for—$10.00 a day. We then formed the Great War Veterans Association (GWVA), with Sgt Harold Mitchell as first President, and began to fight and, with the help of the Women's Patriotic Association (WPA), we began gradually to

The house Howard Leopold Morry built in Ferryland.

Jim Barnable and Howard Morry later in life.

get reforms, better pensions, etc. At present [1950] we are part of the Canadian Legion and, to my mind, have not a thing to grouse about.

There are not many of the first members of that first Veterans Association living now. In fact, the members of the first Newfoundland Regt. are getting scarce, and it gives you a kind of sad feeling when some tottering chap comes up and says "Hello Morry" or whatever your name may be. "How are you, you just look fine, I'd know you anywhere," you shake and tell him the same, though both know we are just old sweats, who have met for the first time after twenty or maybe thirty years, but still the old feeling is there for the chap that went through it with you, and you could depend your life on him in any kind of a do.

I see a few of the old crowd who are bums, but I never pass them by. I knew them for good men once, when men were needed and, after all, who am I to pass judgement on my buddy of former days. Perhaps if I got the same deal he did, I'd be just as lost as him. One thing I notice as I get older, you look more leniently on your fellows' faults and foibles. For you begin to realize your own. The years mellow and, when a bunch meet in the club, why you fast forget you're old and, after a few beers or something, you feel that the world is still a pretty good old place in spite of everything.

The fishing now had changed from oars and sails to motor-boats and, as a result, crews got more fish, but needed more to pay expenses. Still, the fellows that did not get engines backed right out of the picture. For years, the price held up, everyone was beginning to live a little better than before. Then, around 1929 and the early 30's, came the slump, and starvation and broken hearts. Consumption got very prevalent. I knew men to fish day after day, knowing in their hearts that they could not get fish enough to see them through, and guilty enough to keep right on. These years of the thirties did more harm to Newfoundland than can ever be repaired, as far as the fishing population goes. It drove almost every independent and hardworking fisherman away from it, and only left the men with families who could not go and the men who did not care how much fish they got as long as they were sure of the dole. Not a merchant went broke in all those years, but some of our best families left the country they loved so well.

We got Commission of Government, and these English gen-tlemen did a lot for the country and the fishermen, in spite of being led up in Blind Alleys by the merchants. Like getting the Commission to build vessels for the fishermen and giving them to them to clear after so many years, then when they were built, the merchants would not outfit them. And the result, they were a dead loss to the Commission and the people. That is an example of the kind of cooperation the fish merchants gave the Commission of Government in their endeavours to get the people on their feet.

The merchants, in the meantime, founded a fish pool under Government protection, and no one was allowed to sell fish to anyone not belonging to the country, or to export it, unless you had $10,000 to put in the pools. NAFEL they called it [Newfoundland Associated Fish Exporters Limited], *and it did good to them, the merchants, in keeping their prices at a profit-able level for them. They paid as much as five dollars a quintal to the fisherman less than what was paid to the fishermen in*

Halifax. Besides, we had to sell 224 lbs. for a draft of fish or a green quintal as we call it, while our fellow fishermen on the mainland sold 180 lbs. for a draft or a green quintal. So you can see where we got off at $5.00 less for 224 lbs. than they got for 180 (figure it out) and bringing in loads of fish. Still, knowing that, no matter how much they'd catch, they'd be hungry and half naked. I was fortunately a little better off than a good many of my neighbors, having some land and a small pension coming in each month. But I know lots of the best men that ever put foot in a boat having to go look for dole, 65 cents a day per person, and let one try to live on that, and some who kept off the dole lived on less. Not one fish merchant went broke in all these years and they broke lots of independent men and starved them and their families. I myself had a big voyage of fish, all we could handle, in 1930, and had to sell an insurance to pay the men. Fish went down to $3.50 for the best and $1.25 for the West India.

Postscript

After he was invalided out in January of 1917, Howard's comrades-in-arms still had many months of fighting and unrelenting misery ahead of them. Soon after he left for Blighty, the Regiment was back on the Somme and won battle honours at Transloy Ridge in October 1916. Like Gallipoli, however, the Somme was a major defeat overall for both sides, costing hundreds of thousands of lives. In the Spring of 1917, a different approach was attempted at Arras. This was a war of advances rather than trench warfare, and it was here that the Canadian contingent won their greatest honours at Vimy Ridge. A part of this overall theatre of war also saw a tiny number of Newfoundlanders hold off a vastly superior force at Monchy-Le-Preux. But once again, courage and endurance were offset by overall defeat and massive loss of life, with the largest number of RNR men killed since Beaumont-Hamel (166 killed, 141 wounded). The Battle of Arras was one more bitter defeat for the British, who lost in total 160,000 men in the campaign.

Something had to be done to break the stalemate on the western front. The German attempt involved the use of mustard gas, but it proved equally fatal to their own troops due to unpredictable wind shifts. The British option was to involve tanks, a relatively new invention, to shield infantry as they advanced. With this they achieved some measure of success. Beginning on November 20, 1917, Cambrai was one of the first attempts at using this technique, and the RNR was there alongside their British counterparts. During the coming weeks, skirmishes at Marcoing Copse and Masnieres cost the RNR dearly. Once again, the gains in the Battle of Cambrai were more or less counterbalanced by losses, not the least in human life. The RNR suffered 352 casualties and 110 dead. King George was so moved by the valiant and yet largely futile attempts of the small regiment from Newfoundland to play its part in these battles that he awarded the regiment the prefix "Royal," the only regiment to be so honoured while in the field during WWI.

Another bitterly cold and miserable winter lay ahead, and little progress on either side was either attempted or accomplished during those months. When the German forces were encountered again, however, the winds of war had shifted, and the British led forces seemed to have regained their momentum. One after the other, they led battles against the Germans at Keiberg Ridge, Ledeghem, Courtrai, and Lys, all the time with the German forces in retreat. Those few Newfoundlanders who had survived to this point must have felt a rush of pride and hope at playing a part in this succession of victories, after having suffered under so many defeats and stalemates over the previous three years, since landing in Suvla Bay.

Still, by now it was becoming more and more difficult to fill the thinning ranks of the RNR and, in a last ditch attempt to fill the void, conscription was voted in back home on May 18, 1918. Although it was a success in raising the needed conscripts, it was immensely unpopular and, in the event, unnecessary, as none of the conscripts ever saw service overseas due to the cessation of hostilities on November 11, 1918.

The official count of Newfoundland losses in the entire war: 1,570 dead and 2,314 wounded. This from an enlistment of less than 7,000 and a total island population of about 200,000. The social and economic impacts of such losses on Newfoundland were profound. Many believe these losses may have been one of the major causes of the total failure of the Newfoundland economy and its loss of sovereignty, with the eventual need to call on Britain to institute a Commission of Government.

Howard Leopold Morry not only survived the war and the hard times that followed in Newfoundland, but lived to a ripe old age. He died at home in Ferryland on February 8, 1972, just short of his eighty-seventh birthday. The cause of death was aortic stenosis and, though indeed he did suffer all his life from a weak heart, a result of the rheumatic fever he contracted at Ypres, it did not seriously reduce the quality of his life or his joy in it. He lived a full life, raising a family of nine who survived childhood and went on to live long and prosperous lives themselves. Unfortunately, his beloved Scottish lassie, Fredris, was not so fortunate and died in 1948, at the age of only fifty-three. She had never returned to Scotland after the war. Twice they managed to save enough to pay for a return visit, and twice she spent the money on things she thought of greater value to the family, first a piano (she was a virtuoso on it and loved entertaining) and then an automobile, one of the first

(ABOVE & FOLLOWING) *Howard Morry—The life and place he loved.*

on the southern shore. Bill Morry, Howard Morry's eldest son, wrote about this story and published an article entitled "How Mom Got Her Piano" in the St. John's *Evening Telegram* on Wednesday, February 25, 1998.

Despite the difficulties in the fishery described above, Howard was able to partially rebuild the Morry fish business and, later, his son Bill was successful in restoring it to some of its former glory, before the cod fishery collapsed in the 1990s as a consequence of questionable management decisions leading to disastrous overfishing of the stock.

Whether fishing, haying, hauling wood, or telling anyone who would listen about the fascinating history of Ferryland, Howard Morry was never happier than when he was at home in the place he loved and missed so much when he was overseas.

Although he came through the war without receiving a single wound, ironically he went through most of his life with his left hand seriously damaged and missing several digits, as he explained in this snippet from a letter to his daughter Jean:

One morning the ninth of March [ca. 1920], *frosty smoke coming out of the water, I heard the house cracking with the frost (remember Jean), and the wind just light enough to take the slob ice off the land. So I got up and went out on a long point. It was all ice from the sea freezing on it and it took me a long while to crawl out. I got up on the top of a sloping rock, with just room to lie on and piled a few lumps of ice ahead of me so the birds would not see me. I had two guns. The big muzzle loader to fire into the flock and the double barrel 12 gauge hammer gun to shoot the cripples. I put the cartridge gun on the slope of the rock beside me and that's where I made the mistake. I was too careful. If I had cocked her she may not have gone off, as the hammer were lose and when I fired the big gun, I heard her sliding and looked and she was sliding down over the rocks with the muzzle towards me. I knew I was for it and just had time to get on my hands and knees.*

When she went off, it took the coat and shirts and my hand on the far side. Just grazed my stomach. When I saw my mitt going away up in the air I knew my hand was hit and it was a mess. I made for home, with my wrist held tightly to stop the blood. When I came to the cliff, I lay down, for I knew I was due for a reaction and if I fainted going up the cliff, I'd fall. So I just lay there and felt the heat come on me. I got weak. When I came around, the frost had congealed the blood and there was a huge lump of frozen blood on my breast where I had held it against me while I was weak. I climbed the bank and made for the doctors, only to find that he had gone to Cape Broyle on a maternity call. So I came back home and tied it up myself.

Fredris was still asleep. She was expecting in a few weeks and I did not want to give her a shock, so when I went to the bedroom, she woke up and asked me what was wrong. I said I hit my thumb with a hammer. So I took my good clothes and made for Cape Broyle. The doctor tied it up and sent me to hospital, lost the thumb, first finger, and part of the second one. Came home from Hospital on the 18th and walked around for a few days looking at the ducks and moaning. First thing when I got home, I asked Fredris, where's my gun. She said "You're finished with that. I don't want to be worrying about you anymore."

After I was home for a fortnight, one day she brought the guns to me and said, there they are, take them, I can't watch you moaning around. Poor Mom; unknowingly I cost her many anxious hours, when I was away shooting. I did not know till about a couple of years before she died. I had gone shooting on an awful stormy day, early in the morning, and had not come home, and at 4 p.m., when the big kids came home, she came looking for me. I heard someone crying, and I went to the sound, and there she was crying like a baby. I never realized till then how much she must have worried while I was away, and I never gave her anymore worry.

After his wife, Fredris, died, and especially as he got older, Howard took every opportunity he could find to spend time in Scotland. Whether it was the memory of their courting, or those adventurous days when the Newfoundland Regiment garrisoned Edinburgh Castle, he could not seem to ever get enough time to relive those memories, and visited the country again and again, until he was too old to make the journey in his mid-eighties.

Howard was also an avid history buff and particularly worked tirelessly to have due recognition given to the importance of Ferryland in the history of Newfoundland, and indeed all of English North America. Long before the "dig" that now attracts so many visitors to the archeological site at the location of the Colony of Avalon was even being contemplated, Howard was working on everyone from Nimshi Crewe, the sole archivist at the time of Confederation, to Joey Smallwood himself, to raise awareness of the importance of this site.

(ABOVE & FOLLOWING) *Howard Morry on some of his many visits to Scotland. Whether chatting with the lads and lassies in Princes Street in the shadow of Edinburgh Castle, or visiting memorials, such as that to the Royal Scots Fusiliers (companions of the RNR in the trenches), Scotland could truly be called Howard Morry's home away from home.*

178 WHEN THE GREAT RED DAWN IS SHINING

Howard was personally invited to attend the reopening of the Newfoundland Museum on January 21, 1957. Many of the artefacts featured in the historical displays at the reopening were contributed by Howard Morry, from Isle au Bois as well as from the site that he knew to be that of Baltimore's mansion though no scientific evidence of the fact existed at the time.

In recognition of his efforts, he was made an Associate Councillor of the Newfoundland Historical Society in 1961.

Howard remained true to his fellow soldiers, especially those they left behind, and never missed an opportunity to commemorate their sacrifices, in particular making sure that young people understood that while July 1 was a cause for celebration in the rest of Canada, it was a sad day for Newfoundlanders—a day when those who gave their all were to be remembered. My sister, Lanny, tells the story of how, as a cub reporter from the mainland working for the *Daily News*, she was aghast at the sombre atmosphere in downtown St. John's on the 1st of July. Seeing our grandfather among those laying wreaths at the war memorial she confronted him accusingly, saying that this was no way to celebrate Canada's birthday. Dad

Evening Telegram, St. John's, Nfld., Monday, July 14, 1969

Monument unveiled

Harold Morry, Ferryland's oldest war veteran, Saturday unveiled the monument to the colony of Avalon's founder, Lord Baltimore. The monument is a symbol of Baltimore's "mansion house" of stone and timber. Two bronze plaques are fastened to a backing of three white oak timbers. It stands near the site of the original mansion. (Telegram Photo)

Howard Morry unveiling the monument to Lord Baltimore, 1969.

Morry kindly and patiently explained to her the "real" significance of this day, to Newfoundlanders. Lanny never forgot this lesson and attends the daybreak ceremony held by Newfoundlanders at the National War Memorial in Ottawa each July 1.

Although he was invalided out in January of 1917, Howard Morry was entitled to, and received, the following medals for his service: 1914-15 Star plus Riband; Victory Medal; British War Medal; War Badge No. 76. He also proudly retained and treasured the letter, ostensibly signed by King George (though presumably written by one of his secretaries), acknowledging his sacrifices, wishing him a speedy return to health, and thanking him for his service to the "Mother Country."

Medals and memorabilia.

(TOP) *11 Platoon, "C" Company,* RNR *39th reunion of leaving for overseas, February 5, 1954. Back row: Sgt. Charlie Watson, Howard Morry, Bill Buckley, Wilson Loveys, Ned Mansfield. Front row: Sgt. Joe McKinley, Jack Sullivan, Harold Andrews, Chick Duder, Jimmy Lang.*
(BOTTOM) *A Royal Canadian Legion meeting in Chapleau, Ontario, October 1956. Even when travelling, Howard Morry never missed a chance to meet with other veterans, Canadian as well as Newfoundlanders. In this case he was visiting his daughter, Elsie, who had married a Canadian serviceman and moved to northern Ontario after* WWII.

THE DAILY NEW

irst World War veterans of "C"Company New-
oundland Regiment met here Tuesday night for
heir annual reunion and dinner. Two hundred and
orty-four members of the Company landed at Gal-
poli, Sept 20, 1915. Today 103 members are sur-
ving. Chatting over old times here are comrades from
out of town. Left - right: Mont Winsor, Aquaforte
Ferryland; Jack St. John, Topsail; Rev. Louis Head
Comfort Cove; Howard Morry, Ferryland; Roy
Spencer, Fortune; Louis Bartlett, Brigus; and W. M
Walsh, Topsail. (Gordon Morris Photo

(TOP) *44th Annual Reunion of "C" Company, February 1959.*
(BOTTOM) *45th Anniversary of "C" Company Landing at Suvla Bay.*
Those attending and shown in this photograph from the Evening Telegram
include, left to right: Mont Windsor, Jack St. John, Rev. Lewis Head,
Howard Morry, Roy Spencer, Lewis Bartlett, and W.M. Walsh.

Over the years, there have been special occasions on which the events of WWI were especially noted by former RNR members. Dad Morry was always there if health permitted.

In 1961, it was decided to commemorate the 45th Anniversary of the Battle of Beaumont-Hamel by sending a contingent of the survivors and veterans of that dreadful event back to the battlefield for a number of ceremonies between July 1 and 3 of that year. In the end, the survivors were far outnumbered by the "dignitaries," but nevertheless, few of the men would ever have been able to afford a return journey on their own.

Those initially chosen to attend the events in France included: H.K. Goodyear, Neil Patrick, Victor Taylor, Howard Morry, and Roy Spencer. Had it not been for the generosity of Mr. Goodyear in

Survivors of Beaumont-Hamel, forty-five years later. Howard Morry stands centre right in this photograph.

paying his own expenses, one less veteran would have been able to attend. The delegation of those who actually fought at Beaumont-Hamel was rounded out later by Captains George Hicks and Bert Dicks, as well as Charlie Parsons, Ernie Aitken, Joe Goodyear, and A. J. Stacey. Meanwhile the contingent of Canadian dignitaries and press representatives totalled thirty-two, and there were also twenty-three guests representing France.

Strangely, it seems no official report of the visit to Beaumont-Hamel exists, but one of the RNR vets, E. P. Aitken from Deer Lake, became the unofficial reporter for his fellow soldiers and wrote a wonderful, poignant brief of the visit. In it he recorded not just the official ceremonies they attended, but much more importantly the private visits to the graves of brothers in arms. Two of the men present, Ken and Joe Goodyear, sought out the last resting place of their brother Hedley at Le Quesnel Cemetery near Guedecourt where he died. As time was running out and the return journey to Newfoundland was imminent, Ken and Joe Goodyear also rented a cab and rushed to the Cemetery at Bancourt to pay their respects at the grave of another brother, Ray, as well. Regrettably, during this brief visit, they were unable to travel to the grave of a third brother, Stan, who also gave his life in the cause. The incredible losses suffered by this family in the Great War were recorded in the book *The Danger Tree* by David MacFarlane. The entire delegation also visited the trenches and the open terrain in which they had faced the enemy. There they found "rusted steel helmets, some shattered with shrapnel, and bullets, some water bottles and trench mortars." Even then, forty-five years after that desperate and futile battle, there were still in evidence the barbed wire and steel screw posts used to hold the wire entanglements as well as many shell holes, large and small, and of course the "Danger Tree," now encased in cement to preserve it and the memory of the countless soldiers who died there. Aitken notes that at the entrance to the Beaumont-Hamel memorial the words of poet John Oxenham are engraved on a bronze tablet. The first line reads: "Tread softly here—Go reverently and slow." One can imagine that no such imprecation was necessary for these men

1916 and 1961. Veterans V. Taylor, A. Stacey, of St.
John's; Neil Patrick, Corner Brook; Howard Morry, Ferry-
land; Roy Spencer, Fortune; E. Aitken, Deer Lake, Jos.
Goodyear, Grand Falls, pose with Bugler Bernard Evans of
St. John's, serving with the Black Watch in Germany.
Bugler Evans sounded the Last Post during the ceremonies.

THE ONLY HOUSE PAINT with
ΓIIMΓ DΓCICTΛΝΤ DIΛΜΓΝΤC

(TOP) *An official photograph of the delegation. Howard Morry is crouched
on the left behind those seated.* (BOTTOM) *Newspaper article after the
commemorative ceremony at Beaumont-Hamel. From left to right: Victor
Taylor, Anthony Stacey, Neil Patrick, Howard Morry, bugler Bernard
Evans, Roy Spencer, Ernest Aitken, and Josiah Goodyear.*

who were returning to the scene of the most horrific and indelible memory already engraved in their hearts and souls.

After this once in a lifetime chance to revisit the old battlefields, Howard Morry continued his faithful involvement in all activities arranged to commemorate the men who fought, and especially those who did not return.

The fifty-fifth reunion of landing at Suvla Bay, held in 1970, was perhaps the last reunion Howard Morry attended. He was then eighty-five years old and beginning to feel the wear. He died two years later on February 8, 1972.

Dad Morry died as he would have wanted to, at home and at peace in his beloved Ferryland. He received a simple burial, without the pomp and circumstance of the military honours to which he was entitled, and is buried beside his darling Scottish lassie, Fredris, in the Holy Trinity Cemetery in Ferryland, rather than in one of the many "Fields of Honour" in Newfoundland, where he might have chosen

In September of 1964, RNR veterans turned out for their fiftieth anniversary of departure. The timing of the reunion was not exact, but this meeting coincided with the visit of the Princess Royal (Countess of Harewood), Colonel in Chief of the Regiment. Among those shown, back row: Howard Morry (age 79), George Stone, Harold Andrews, Mont Windsor, George Chaulker, Roy Spencer. Front row on right: Fred Waterman. Others unknown.

to be buried. It is in keeping with the way he led his life, both during the war, when he refused to take stripes which would set him apart from his chums, and in his private life after the war, when he aspired not to re-establish the Morry tradition as leading merchants in this little community, but to be one amongst many along with the people whose friendship meant so much to him.

Despite his unassuming manner, or perhaps because of it, he will long be remembered by future generations of family and friends. It is my fondest

MORRY — Passed peacefully away at Ferryland, in his 88th year, Howard L. Morry. Leaving to mourn four sons and four daughters: Phyllis at St. John's, Bill at Ferryland, Tom at Ottawa, Reg at Belleville, Ont., Jean at Utah, U.S.A., Elsie at Sudbury, Ont., Catherine at Los Angeles, U.S.A., and Howard at Kilbride; also one sister Trix in Dartmouth, N.S.; 28 grandchildren, 14 great-grandchildren. Remains resting at Carnell's Funeral Home. Burial to take place at 2:30 p.m. Thursday, January 10th, at the R.C. Parish, Ferryland. Howard Morry served in the Royal Nfld. Regiment during World War I and was a surviver of the July Drive.
feb9,2i

A simple epitaph to a simple man.

hope that, by publishing his memoirs, I am helping a little to honour his memory and to preserve it and to keep his spirit alive.

An old soldier at peace.

Appendix 1

Index of Soldiers Who Fought Alongside Howard Morry

Aitken, Ernest Peyton. Sgt.
Ernest (Ernie) Peyton Aitken,
Regt. #643. *184, 185*
Andrews, Harold. Pte. Harold
James Andrews, Regt. #777;
Wounded at Beaumont-
Hamel. *43, 51, 66, 67, 74, 75,
76, 122, 126, 147, 181, 186*

Barnable, John Joseph (Jack).
Pte. John Joseph Barnable,
Regt. #3027. *20, 21, 165*
Barrett, Harold George. 2nd
Lieut. Harold George Barrett,
Regt. #798: Wounded at
Beaumont-Hamel; Awarded
Military Medal for valour at
Gueudecourt; Died in battle
August 16, 1917. *45, 95, 96, 98*
Bartlett, Lewis G. Sgt. Lewis G.
Bartlett, Regt. #644. *182*

Bernard, Adolph Ernest. Capt.
Adolph Ernest Bernard,
Granted Commission;
Captain, September 21,
1914; British Mediterranean
Expeditionary Force, August
20, 1915; Evacuated Suvla,
sick, December 12, 1915;
Admitted to hospital, Malta,
December 17, 1915; Invalided
to England, January 25, 1916;
Awarded Military Cross,
June 3, 1916; Mentioned in
dispatches, July 11, 1916;
Attached to depot, Ayr, July
12, 1916; Major, October 5,
1916; British Expeditionary
Force, December 1, 1916;
Decorated with Croix de
Guerre, September 1917;
Took command of First

Newfoundland Battalion, June 1, 1918; Returned to UK for special officers' course, June 30, 1918; Returned to BEF, September 29, 1918; Rejoined Battalion, October 6, 1918; Assumed command of First Newfoundland Battalion, March 16, 1919; Embarked for Newfoundland, May 22, 1919; Acting Lieutenant-Colonel, January 1, 1919; Retired July 29, 1919. *41, 43, 50, 51, 82*

Brown, James Michael (Gravy). Likely Pte. James Michael Brown, Regt. #1328; Died in battle December 3, 1915. *77, 89*

Buckley, William. Sgt. William (Bill) Buckley, Regt. #752; Died on October 15, 1955. *181*

Carew, David (Davey). Pte. David Michael Carew, Regt. #776; Killed at Gallipoli, October 7, 1915. *38, 65, 75, 76, 77*

Carew, Victor. Pte. Victor Adrian Carew, Regt. #1560; Died November 20, 1917; Dad Morry's second cousin. *136, 137, 139*

Carew, Vincent. Pte. Vincent Mary Carew, Regt. #3140; Died in battle October 10. 1917 (almost a year to the day after enlisting, but only 8 days after going onto the front line); Brother of Victor (above) but did not serve beside his brother or his cousin, Howard Morry. *139*

Carter, Cyril. Lieut. Cyril B. Carter of St. John's; A distant cousin of Howard Morry's. *77, 78, 89*

Carter, James Henry. L. Cpl. James Henry Carter, Regt. #222, of St. John's; Died in battle (Marcoing Copse) the same day as Vincent Carew above, November 20. 1917; A distant cousin of Howard Morry and apparently served in entirely different platoons and companies as he is not mentioned in the diaries. *139*

Cayley, D. E. Major General D.E. Cayley. No greater tribute could be paid any unit than that contained in the words of Cayley, commanding the Twenty-Ninth Division: "They can look back on a record of which they and their fellow-countrymen have every right to be proud." (From *The First Five Hundred* by Richard Cramm). *82, 88, 96, 107, 112, 153*

Chaulker, George C. Pte. George C, Chaulker, Regt. #1736. *186*

Cleary, Charles Allen. CQMS Charles Allen Cleary, Regt. #679; Died July 1, 1916; Buried Knightsbridge. *138*

Coady, Andrew. Pte. Andrew Coady, Regt. #775. *165*

Coombes, Archibald. The man Coombes mentioned by Howard Morry was possibly Pte. Archibald Coombs,

Regt. #492; Enlisted Sept. 11,
1914; British Mediterranean
Expeditionary Force August
20, 1915; Evacuated Suvla, sick,
November 28, 1915; Rejoined
Battalion, Suez, March 1, 1916;
British Expeditionary Force,
March 14, 1916; Wounded
at Beaumont-Hamel, July 1,
1916; Invalided to England,
July 8, 1916; Repatriated to
Newfoundland, Sept. 13,
1917; Discharged St. John's,
medically unfit, February 14,
1918. *165*

Costello, Daniel (Dan). Pte.
Daniel Stephen Costello, Regt.
#860; Wounded at Beaumont-
Hamel. *66, 114*

Crane, Joseph (Joe). Pte. Joseph
Crane, Regt. #2313; Died
April 14, 1917. *128*

Davis, John (Jack). Pte. John
Davis , Regt. #738; Military
Medal; Answered roll call
after Beaumont-Hamel and
survived the war. *75, 114, 149,
150, 152*

Davis, Walter (Watty). Pte.
Walter Davis, Regt. #5520, Safe
Harbour, Bonavista Bay. *114*

De Lacey, Leo Francis. Sgt. Leo
Francis De Lacey, Regt. #1373,
of St. John's. *139, 147, 149, 150*

Devereaux, John William. L/Cpl.
John (Jack) William Devereaux,
Regt. #3152; Died of complica-
tions related to his wounds on
April 17, 1920. *20, 21*

Donnelly, James J. Capt. James J.
Donnelly; Awarded Military
Cross at Caribou Hill; Died
in battle October 12 1916. *40,
61, 66, 78, 120, 141, 142*

Downey, Michael (Mike). Pte.
Michael Downey, Regt. #862.
40, 77, 89, 165

Duder, Charles R. Pte. Charles
R. (Chick) Duder, Regt. #668.
181

Dunphy, John. Likely Pte. John
Dunphy, Regt. #44; Enlisted
September 2, 1914; British
Mediterranean Expeditionary
Force, August 20, 1915;
Killed in Action, Suvla Bay,
December 12, 1915. *89*

Edgar, Charles LeGallais
(Charlie). 2nd Lieut. Charles
LeGallais Edgar, Regt.
#199; Killed in action,
Sailly-Saillisel, February
26, 1917: Enlisted Sept. 4,
1914; Lance Corporal, April
8, 1915; Corporal, July 27,
1915; British Mediterranean
Expeditionary Force,
August 20, 1915; Acting
Company Quartermaster
Sergeant, November 11,
1915; Sergeant, November
14, 1915; Wounded, Suvla
Bay, December 5, 1915;
Discharged to duty, Jan. 19,
1916; Confirmed to Rank of
Company Quartermaster
Sergeant, January 31, 1916;
British Expeditionary

Force, March 14, 1916; 2nd
Lieutenant, June 5, 1916;
Returned to Newfoundland
on duty, July 11, 1916;
Embarked for UK, August
28, 1916; Returned to BEF,
October 27, 1916; Killed
in action, Sailly-Saillisel,
February 26, 1917. *114*

Edgar, Edwin (Ned). Pte. Edwin
Edgar, Regt. #737; Died July 1,
1916; Buried Memorial Park.
89, 114, 135

Freebairn, Buchanan W. (Chan).
Pte. Buchanan W. Freebairn,
Regt. #724; Died October 23,
1915. *76, 77*

Fitzgerald, John. Pte. John
Fitzgerald, Regt. #295;
Enlisted, September 8,
1914; British Mediterranean
Expeditionary Force, August
20, 1915; Killed in action,
Suvla, December 1, 1915;
Mentioned in dispatches,
London Gazette, July 11,
1916. *80*

Gladney, James Joseph (Jim).
Pte. James Joseph Gladney,
Regt. #771. *41, 79, 114*

Goodyear, Harold K. Lieut.
Harold K. (Ken) Goodyear,
Regt. #1193. *183, 184*

Goodyear, Hedley John. Lieut.
Hedley John Goodyear,
102nd Battalion (Canadian
Expeditionary Force); Died
August 22, 1918. *184*

Goodyear, Josiah Robert. Capt.
Josiah (Joe) Robert Goodyear,
Regt. #573. *184, 185*

Goodyear, Oswald Raymond.
L/Cpl. Oswald Raymond
(Ray) Goodyear, Regt. #2156
(Canadian Expeditionary
Force); Died October 12,
1916. *184*

Goodyear, Stanley C. Lieut.
Stanley (Stan) C., Regt. #334;
Died October 10, 1917. *184*

Gough, Ralph. Probably Pte.
Ralph Gough, Regt. #781,
though Dad Morry spelled the
surname "Goff." *87*

Grant, William Hayes. 2ⁿᵈ Lieut.
William Hayes Grant, Regt.
#410; Enlisted, September
11, 1914; Lance Corporal,
May 21, 1915; 2nd Lieutenant
October 16, 1915; British
Expeditionary Force, March
23, 1916; Killed in action,
in the line near Beaumont-
Hamel, July 16, 1916, aged
25; Buried at Auchonvillers
Military Cemetery. *147*

Green, Patrick (Paddy). Pte.
Patrick Green, Regt. #1055;
Wounded at Beaumont-
Hamel but survived the war.
83, 86, 134

Greene, Walter Martin. Lieut.
Walter Martin Greene, Regt.
#266; Enlisted, September
2, 1914; Lance Corporal,
September 21, 1914; Cor-
poral, November 13, 1914;
Provost Sergeant, April 23,

1915; British Mediterranean Expeditionary Force, August 20, 1915; Awarded Distinguished Conduct Medal, January 24, 1916; British Expeditionary Force, March 14, 1916; 2nd Lieutenant, June 5, 1916; Wounded, Somme Raid, June 28, 1916: Invalided to England, July 5, 1916; Returned to BEF, May 4, 1917; Lieutenant, November 1, 1917; Killed in action, Marcoing, November 20, 1917. *43, 44, 98*

Guy, Mark. Pte. Mark Guy, Regt. #1271; Wounded Beaumont-Hamel. *152, 153*

Hadow, Arthur, L. Lt. Col. Arthur L. Hadow, CMG, MID [2]. *xvii, 94-95, 107, 112-113, 115, 117, 121, 138, 153*

Hannaford, John Joseph. L/Cpl. John Joseph Hannaford, Regt. #792; Wounded at Beaumont-Hamel but survived the war; Howard Morry was Regt. #726, so they must have enlisted the same day or very nearly. *71*

Harvey, William Thomas (Tom). Possibly Pte. William Thomas Harvey, Regt. #751. *83, 86*

Head, Lewis. Sgt. Lewis Head, Regt. #743; Wounded at Beaumont-Hamel. *41, 65, 80, 147, 182*

Higgins, Edmund James (Ed). Sgt. Edmund James Higgins,

Regt. #756; Died, of wounds received at Beaumont-Hamel, on July 2, 1916. *66*

Howard, James John (Jimmy). Pte. James John Howard, Regt. #560; Enlisted, September 16, 1914; British Mediterranean Expeditionary Force, 1915; British Expeditionary Force, March 14, 1916; Killed in Action, Beaumont-Hamel, July 1, 1916, aged 22; Buried Memorial Park. *136*

Janes, Frederick (Fred). L./Cpl. Frederick Janes, Regt. #1275; Killed at Beaumont-Hamel. *66*

Kent, Martin Patrick. L/Cpl. Martin Patrick Kent, Regt. #1270; Died October 12, 1916. *145*

Lang, James Patrick. 2nd Lieut. James (Jimmy) Patrick Lang, Regt. #870. *89, 181*

Le Messurier, Francis Ernest (Frank). Sgt. Francis Ernest Le Messurier, Regt. #632; Wounded at Beaumont-Hamel; Married to Helena Morry, Howard Morry's first cousin once removed. *61, 69*

Le Messurier, Philip Sorsoleil. Lieut. Philip Sorsoleil Le Messurier, Regt. #62; Wounded Suvla, November 23, 1915. After recovering, he rose through the ranks to Lieutenant, not a common occurrence; Very remotely related to Howard Morry. *69*

Loveys, Aubrey Wilson. S/Sgt. Aubrey Wilson Loveys, Regt. #827. *181*

Mansfield, Edward. L/Cpl. Edward (Ned) Mansfield, Regt. #749. *181*

McDonald, Patrick Q. (Paddy). Cpl. Patrick Q. McDonald Regt. #230; Enlisted, September 2, 1914; British Expeditionary Force, December 12, 1916; Wounded, Broembeek, October 9, 1917; Invalided to England, October 19, 1917; Attached to Depot, Ayr, November 28, 1917; Lance-Corporal, January 11, 1918; Awarded Military Medal, January 14, 1918; Acting Corporal, March 19, 1918; Returned to Newfoundland, furlough, July 21, 1918; Embarked for UK, October 19, 1918; Demobilized, UK, March 6, 1919. *138-139*

McKinley, Joseph (Joe). CQMS Joseph McKinley, Regt. #748; Wounded at Beaumont-Hamel. *36, 41, 66, 135, 181*

McNeil, Hector. Capt. Hector McNeil Regt. #31; Enlisted, September 2, 1914; Regimental Quartermaster Sergeant, September 21, 1914; British Mediterranean Expeditionary Force,

August 20, 1915: British Expeditionary Force, March 14, 1916; Acting Quartermaster, July 12, 1916; Hon. Lieutenant Quartermaster, November 26, 1916; Captain Quartermaster, July 23, 1918: Embarked for Newfoundland, furlough, July 24, 1918; Returned to UK, November 27, 1918; Returned to British Expeditionary Force, December 8, 1918; Mentioned in despatches, March 16, 1919; Awarded OBE, June 3, 1919. *83, 85, 86*

Mifflin, Henry (Harry). Sgt. Henry Mifflin, Regt. #742. *41, 65, 66, 67, 94, 147*

Mitchell, Harold. Sgt. Harold Mitchell, Regt. #828. *75, 167*

Moore, Daniel (Dan). Pte. Daniel Joseph Moore, Regt. #741. *80, 83, 94, 166*

Murphy, Joachim. Pte. Joachim Murphy, Regt. #696; Died November 7 1915. *41, 78*

Myers, Albert (Abe or Pigshit). Pte.. Albert Myers, Regt. #1367. *147*

O'Flynn, Michael Joseph (Mike). Pte. Michael Joseph O'Flynn, Regt. #727; Died July 1, 1916; Buried in Memorial Park; Referred to in Dad Morry's memoirs as "Mike Flynn". *136*

O'Neil, Frederick Michael (Fred). Pte. Frederick Michael

O'Neil, Regt. #402; Enlisted, September 8, 1914; British Mediterranean Expeditionary Force, August 20, 1915; British Expeditionary Force, March 14, 1916; Admitted Hospital, Marseilles, March 22, 1916; Discharged from Hospital, April 6, 1916; Wounded, Somme Raid, June 28, 1916; Invalided to England, July 1, 1916; Attached to Depot, Ayr, August 15, 1916; Embarked for Newfoundland, September 27, 1916; Discharged, St. John's, medically unfit, January 31, 1917; Mentioned in despatches, April 9, 1917. *134*

Parsons, Charles H. (Charlie). The Charlie Parsons mentioned who survived Beaumont-Hamel is probably Pte. Charles H. Parsons, Regt. #1708; Died October 19, 1918. *138, 141, 184*

Patrick, Neil. R S M Neil Patrick, Regt. #51. *183, 185*

Penney, Josiah H. (Joe). Pte. Josiah H. Penney, Regt. #665; Died July 1, 1916, aged 26; Buried Memorial Park. *136*

Phillips, George Gordon. 2ⁿᵈ Lt. George Gordon Phillips, Regt. #1164; Died October 12, 1916; Received the Military Medal and the Russian Order of St. George for courageous conduct. *134*

Quigley, Michael J. Pte. Michael J. Quigley, Regt. #861; Died July 1, 1916, aged 27; Buried Y Ravine. *138*

Rendell, Clifford (Cliff). 2ⁿᵈ Lt. Clifford Rendell, Regt. #621; Died in battle July 22, 1916, aged 21; Buried at Etaples Military Cemetery. *126*

Roper, Henry (Hal). Pte. Henry Roper, Regt. #670. *102*

Rowsell, Reginald S. We know this was Capt. Reginald S. Rowsell, Military Cross, killed in action April 14, 1917, because Howard Morry mentions later that he died in action. The other Capt. Rowsell, Capt. Arthur Rowsell, Regt. #2491, survived the war. *48, 98, 99, 135, 141, 142, 152-153*

Sheehan, John Joseph (Joe). Sgt. John Joseph Sheehan, Regt. #35; Enlisted, September 2, 1914; British Mediterranean Expeditionary Force, August 20, 1915; British Expeditionary Force, March 14, 1916; Wounded, Beaumont-Hamel, July 1, 1916; Invalided to England, July 5, 1916; Lance Corporal, October 27, 1916; Returned to British Expeditionary Force, December 30, 1916; Corporal, February 9, 1917; Wounded, Sailly-Saillisel, February 24,

1917; Discharged, medically unfit, December 8, 1917; Enlisted Newfoundland Forestry Battalion, December 11, 1917; Sergeant, December 12, 1917; Embarked for UK, December 21, 1917; Died of pneumonia, December 28, 1917. His name is misspelled "Shaheen" in Howard Morry's memoir. *128*

Shiwak, John. L/Cpl. John Shiwak, Regt. #1735; Died in battle, November 20, 1917. *128-129*

Short, William (Billy). Possibly 2/Lt. William Short, Regt. #878. *76*

Snow, William (Bill). Pte. William Snow, Regt. #750; Died October 12, 1916. *78*

Soper, Morley. Pte. Morley Soper, Regt. #1259; Died December 29, 1915. *77, 97*

Spencer, Roy. Pte. Roy Spencer, Regt. #859. *74, 182, 183, 185, 186*

Stacey, Anthony James. Sgt. Anthony James Stacey, Regt. #466. *xx, 184, 185*

St. John, John. Pte. John (Jack) St. John, Regt. #673. *116, 182*

Stone, George J. Pte. George J. Stone, Regt. #772. *186*

Sullivan, John T. L/Cpl. John (Jack) T. Sullivan, Regt. #769. *181*

Summers, Michael Francis. The "Capt. Somers" mentioned must be Captain Michael Francis Summers (there was no Capt. Somers at Beaumont-Hamel); Appointed Quarter Master, September 21, 1914; British Mediterranean Expeditionary Force, August 20, 1915; Captain, November 23, 1915; British Expeditionary Force, March 14, 1916; Wounded, Beaumont-Hamel, July 1, 1916; Died of wounds, July 16, 1916. Buried Gezaincourt Communal Cemetery Extension. *102, 103, 138*

Taylor, Victor G. CQMS Victor G. Taylor, Regt. #111. *183, 185*

Thomas, Walter (Watty). Pte. Walter Thomas, Regt. #722; Died, of wounds received at Beaumont-Hamel, on July 15, 1916. *65–66*

Viguers, William (Bill). Pte. William Viguers, Regt. #1171; Wounded at Beaumont-Hamel. *61*

Walsh, William. Pte. William Walsh, Regt. #683. *182*

Watson, James (Charlie). Most likely CQMS James Watson, Regt. #2406; Meritorious Service medal; Mentioned in Dispatches. He was born in Scotland. *66, 181*

White, Willis. Pte. Willis White, Regt. #739; Died at Beaumont-Hamel. *41, 65, 87, 89, 147*

Winsor, Stanley Charles (Stan). L./Cpl. Stanley Charles Winsor, Regt. #301; Wounded at both Gallipoli and Steenbeke and eventually invalided out in 1917; Howard Morry's second cousin, once removed; brother of Mont (below). *20, 21*

Windsor, Wilfred Montgomery (Mont). CQMS Wilfred Montgomery Windsor, Regt. #672; Howard Morry's second cousin once removed, and lifelong best friends; Brother of Stan (above). *34, 68, 69, 86, 160, 182, 186*

Appendix 2

Morry Family Tree

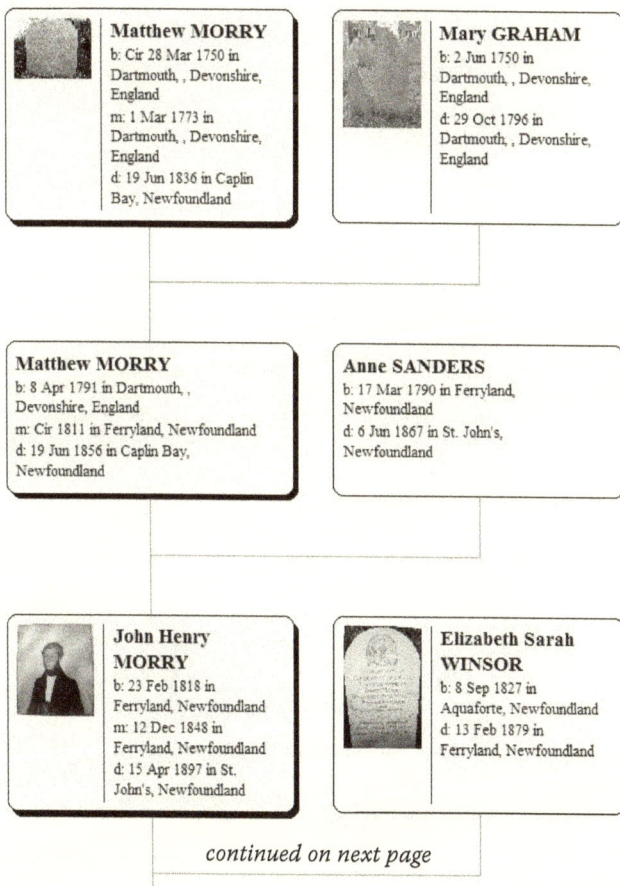

Matthew MORRY
b: Cir 28 Mar 1750 in Dartmouth, , Devonshire, England
m: 1 Mar 1773 in Dartmouth, , Devonshire, England
d: 19 Jun 1836 in Caplin Bay, Newfoundland

Mary GRAHAM
b: 2 Jun 1750 in Dartmouth, , Devonshire, England
d: 29 Oct 1796 in Dartmouth, , Devonshire, England

Matthew MORRY
b: 8 Apr 1791 in Dartmouth, , Devonshire, England
m: Cir 1811 in Ferryland, Newfoundland
d: 19 Jun 1856 in Caplin Bay, Newfoundland

Anne SANDERS
b: 17 Mar 1790 in Ferryland, Newfoundland
d: 6 Jun 1867 in St. John's, Newfoundland

John Henry MORRY
b: 23 Feb 1818 in Ferryland, Newfoundland
m: 12 Dec 1848 in Ferryland, Newfoundland
d: 15 Apr 1897 in St. John's, Newfoundland

Elizabeth Sarah WINSOR
b: 8 Sep 1827 in Aquaforte, Newfoundland
d: 13 Feb 1879 in Ferryland, Newfoundland

continued on next page

from previous page

Thomas Graham MORRY
b: 4 Dec 1849 in Ferryland, Newfoundland
m: 1 Jun 1880 in Renews, Newfoundland
d: 24 Jul 1935 in Victoria, British Columbia, Canada

Catherine Frances WHITE
b: 20 Aug 1852 in Ferryland, Newfoundland
d: 27 Aug 1927 in Mount Pearl, Newfoundland

Howard Leopold MORRY
b: 24 Jul 1885 in Ferryland, Newfoundland
m: 2 Jun 1915 in Edinburgh, , Midlothian, Scotland
d: 8 Feb 1972 in Ferryland, Newfoundland, Canada

Fredris Marion Powdrell MINTY
b: 3 Apr 1895 in Edinburgh, , Midlothian, Scotland
d: 15 Feb 1948 in Ferryland, Newfoundland

Thomas Graham MORRY
b: 4 Dec 1919 in Ferryland, Newfoundland
m: 6 Sep 1945 in St. John's, Newfoundland
d: 1 May 2008 in Ottawa, , Ontario, Canada

Evelyn Mary WHEELER
b: 6 Nov 1917 in St. John's, Newfoundland
d: 2 Aug 2009 in Ottawa, , Ontario, Canada

Christopher John MORRY
b: 25 May 1949 in St. John's, Newfoundland, Canada

Photo Credits

Page iii. Howard Morry Memorabilia Shadow Box. Courtesy Howard Glendon Morry.

Page vi. "When the Great Red Dawn Is Shining" postcard. Originally printed in England by Bamforth and Co. Ltd., 1917. From the collection of Christopher Morry.

Page xxvii. Howard Leopold Morry and his diaries. Photo collage by Christopher Morry.

Page 3. Portrait of John Henry Morry. Photo by Christopher Morry used by permission of Edward Thompson.

Page 4. The Holdsworth House. Centre for Newfoundland Studies, Memorial University, St. John's, NL.

Page 5. Thomas Graham Morry in Fort Garry during the Northwest Rebellion. From Howard Leopold Morry's scrapbook.

Page 9. Catherine and Thomas Morry with Trix, Bert, Howard, and Graham, ca. 1892. Photo courtesy Fredris Mercer Caines.

Page 11. Morry family, ca. 1900. Photo courtesy Karen Funkhouser Chapman.

Page 15. Howard Leopold Morry in St. John's, ca. 1903. Photo courtesy Karen Funkhouser Chapman.

Page 21. Howard Morry with Jack Devereaux and Stan Windsor. Photo courtesy Fredris Mercer Caines.

Page 21. Photos of John Joseph (Jack) Barnable. Photos courtesy Steve Barnable.

Page 22. Howard Leopold Morry (marked with an X) in Standard Regimental Platoon Photograph, ca. 1915. From Howard Leopold Morry's scrapbook.

Page 22. Howard Leopold Morry and a fellow recruit in St. John's, winter 1914-15. Photo courtesy Fredris Mercer Caines.

Page 22. A staged photograph before leaving St. John's. Photo courtesy Fredris Mercer Caines.

Page 25. The "Trail of the Caribou." Image from *The Newfoundland Regiment and the Great War* (http://www.therooms. ca/regiment/part2_trail_of_the_ caribou.asp). Used by permission of The Rooms, St. John's, NL.

Page 27. Howard Morry's platoon in "C" Company. Photo courtesy Fredris Mercer Caines.

Page 27. Howard and other recruits and well-wishers in St. John's before boarding. Photo courtesy Beatrice Morry Giovannetti.

Page 28. The *Neptune* boarding members of the RNR in St. John's harbour. From the collection of the late Elsie Morry Ranger, courtesy of Christine and Denis Blake.

Page 29. Howard Leopold Morry and mates on leave in Edinburgh. Photo courtesy Fredris Mercer Caines.

Page 31. Instructions on how to get paid. From Howard Leopold Morry's scrapbook.

Page 32. Instructions for use and care of tube helmets. From Howard Leopold Morry's scrapbook.

Page 33. An insert from a "package of fags." From Howard Leopold Morry's scrapbook.

Page 34. Private Howard Leopold Morry, "C" Company, RNR, in Edinburgh shortly after arrival at the same time wedding photographs were taken on June 3, 1915. Photo courtesy Karen Funkhouser Chapman.

Page 35. Fredris Minty with her sister, Mary, in Edinburgh, ca. April-May, 1915. Photo courtesy Fredris Mercer Caines.

Page 40. Tents of the Newfoundland Regiment at Stobs Camp, Scotland, May 1915. Provincial Archives Division of The Rooms (PANL VA37-17), St. John's, NL.

Page 40. Presentation of colours to RNR at Stobs Camp, June 10, 1915. From Howard Leopold Morry's scrapbook. Provincial Archives Division of The Rooms (VA 40-20.4), St. John's, NL.

Page 41. Howard Morry's squad at Stobs Camp, May 28, 1915. From the collection of the late Elsie Morry Ranger, courtesy of Christine and Denis Blake.

Page 42. Two forged passes. From Howard Leopold Morry's scrapbook.

Page 44. Two legitimate passes. From Howard Leopold Morry's scrapbook.

Page 46. Banns and marriage certificate. St. Michael's Presbyterian Church, Edinburgh, June 2, 1915. From Howard Leopold Morry's scrapbook.

Page 47. Wedding photograph of Fredris Minty and Howard Leopold Morry. Photo courtesy Karen Funkhouser Chapman.

Page 49. Postcard from Howard Leopold Morry to his father, dated June 22, 1915. Courtesy Fredris Mercer Caines.

Page 51. Harold Andrews and Howard Morry before departing Britain. Photo courtesy Fredris Mercer Caines.

Page 52. Howard Morry and mates just before departing Britain. Photo courtesy Peter Morry.

Page 59. Newfoundland Regiment Drum and Bugle Band, Aldershot, England, 1915. Provincial Archives of Newfoundland and Labrador (PANL B-3-21), St. John's, NL.

Page 60. The SS *Megantic* as it appeared when in use as a troop carrier. Photo from *Newfoundland's Grand Banks* website (http://ngb. chebucto,org/).

Page 67. Harold Mifflin and Harold Andrews. Photo courtesy Fredris Mercer Caines.

Page 69. Photo of CQMS. Wilfred Montgomery Windsor courtesy Dorothy Windsor Keough. Photo of L. Cpl. Stanley Charles Windsor from *Newfoundland's Grand Banks* website. Photo of Pvt. Francis Ernest Le Messurier (at Stobs Camp) courtesy Victoria Le Messurier Badcock. Photo of Lieut. Philip Sorsoleil Le Messurier from *Newfoundland's Grand Banks* website.

Page 90. Howard Morry's father, Thomas Graham Morry, and first child, Phyllis. Photo courtesy Fredris Mercer Caines.

Page 99. Cape Helles British Headquarters. From *Newfoundland and the Great War* (www.heritage.nf.ca).

Page 123. Diagram of the SAP trenches. From Howard Leopold Morry's scrapbook.

Page 139. Three who didn't make it. Photos of Victor and Vincent Carew courtesy Ida White Michael. Photo of L. Cpl. James Carter from *Newfoundland's Grand Banks* website.

Page 140. Propaganda message following the defeat at the Somme. From Howard Leopold Morry's scrapbook.

Page 141. A page from Howard Morry's paybook. Courtesy Howard Glendon Morry.

Page 142. Photo of Captain James Donnelly from *Newfoundland's Grand Banks* website. Photo of Lamont Paterson, Arthur Raley, Walter Frederick Rendell, and Reginald S. Rowsell from *Newfoundland's Grand Banks* website.

Page 149. Photo of Leo De Lacey, Howard Morry, and Jack Davis—survivors of the Battle of Beaumont-Hamel. From the collection of the late Elsie Morry Ranger, courtesy Christine and Denis Blake.

Page 150. The Second Newfoundland Regiment forming in St. John's, Summer of 1916. From Howard Leopold Morry's scrapbook.

Page 155. Howard Morry's depiction of the Ypres Salient, redrawn by Christopher Morry from a diagram in the original diaries of Howard Leopold Morry.

Page 161. Emily Frances Victoria Morry (Fanny). Photo courtesy Beatrice Morry Giovannetti.

Page 162. Furlough from Wandsworth Hospital, October 16, 1916. From Howard Leopold Morry's scrapbook.

Page 163. James and Nellie Minty. Photos courtesy Karen Funkhouser Chapman.

Page 164. The ticket home. From Howard Leopold Morry's scrapbook.

Page 164. Postcard of SS Scandinavian given to passengers by Allen Line ships, from the collection of Christopher Morry.

Page 167. The house Howard Leopold Morry built in Ferryland. Photo by Howard Leopold Morry.

Page 168. Jim Barnable and Howard Morry later in life. From Howard Leopold Morry's photo album.

Page 173/4. Howard Morry—The life and place he loved. Four photos from Howard Leopold Morry's photo album.

Page 177/8. Howard Morry on some of his many visits to Scotland. Four photos from Howard Leopold Morry's photo album.

Page 179. Howard Morry unveiling the monument to Lord Baltimore, 1969. Clipping from the *Evening Telegram* July 14, 1969, from Howard Leopold Morry's scrapbook. Courtesy *The Telegram*.

Page 180. Medals and memorabilia. Photo of medals courtesy Howard Ian Morry. Photo of memorabilia courtesy Howard Glendon Morry.

Page 181. 11 Platoon, "C" Company, RNR 39th reunion of leaving for overseas, February 5, 1954. From Howard Leopold Morry's scrapbook.

Page 181. A Royal Canadian Legion meeting in Chapleau, Ontario, October 1956. From Howard Leopold Morry's scrapbook.

Page 182. 44th Annual Reunion of "C" Company, February 1959. Clipping from the St. John's *Daily News* (February 1959) from Howard Leopold Morry's scrapbook.

Page 182. 45th Anniversary of "C" Company Landing at Suvla Bay. Clipping from the *Evening Telegram* September 1960 from Howard Leopold Morry's scrapbook. Courtesy *The Telegram*.

Page 183. Survivors of Beaumont-Hamel, forty-five years later. From Howard Leopold Morry's scrapbook.

Page 185. An official photograph of the delegation. From Howard Leopold Morry's scrapbook.

Page 185. Newspaper article after the commemorative ceremony at Beaumont-Hamel. Clipping from the *Evening Telegram* July 1961 from Howard Leopold Morry's scrapbook. Courtesy *The Telegram*.

Page 186. In September of 1964, RNR veterans turned out for their fiftieth anniversary of departure. From Howard Leopold Morry's scrapbook.

Page 187. A simple epitaph to a simple man. Obituary for Howard Leopold Morry. Clipping from the *Evening Telegram* February 9-10, 1972, from Karen Funkhouser Chapman. Courtesy *The Telegram*.

Page 187. An old soldier at peace. Photo courtesy Karen Funkhouser Chapman.

References

This is a bibliography of published titles pertaining to the Royal Newfoundland Regiment in WWI, including non-fiction works only and excluding fictional narratives, film documentaries, television and radio productions, theses, and term papers. To my knowledge, this is a complete and comprehensive list.

Browne, Gary, and Darrin McGrath. *Soldier Priest in the Killing Fields of Europe: Padre Thomas Nangle Chaplain to the Newfoundland Regiment in WW1*. St. John's: DRC Publishers, 2006.

Browne, Gary. *Forget-Me-Not: Fallen Boy Soldiers*. St. John's: DRC Publishers, 2010.

Cave, Joy B. *What Became of Corporal Pittman?* St. John's: Breakwater Books, 1976.

Christie, N. M. *For King and Empire: The Newfoundlanders in the Great War, the Western Front 1916-1918*. Ottawa: CEF Books, 2003.

Cramm, Richard. *The First Five Hundred: Being a Historical Sketch of the Military Operations of the Royal Newfoundland Regiment in Gallipoli and on the Western Front*. Albany, New York: C.F. Williams & Son, Inc., 1921.

Facey-Crowther, David R., ed. *Better Than the Best: The Story of the Royal Newfoundland Regiment, 1795-1995*. St. John's: Royal Newfoundland Regiment Advisory Council, 1995.

Facey-Crowther, David R., ed., and James Steele. *Lieutenant Owen William Steele of the Newfoundland Regiment: Diary and Letters*. Montréal: McGill-Queen's University Press, 2003.

Fitzgerald, Jack. *The Spring Rice Document: Newfoundland at War 1914-1918*. St. John's: Creative Book Publishing, 2011.

Gallishaw, John. *Trenching at Gallipoli: The Personal Narrative of a Newfoundlander with the Ill-fated Dardanelles Expedition*. New York: The Century Co., 1916. Reprinted by DRC Publishing in 2005.

Gogos, Frank, and Morgan MacDonald. *Known unto God: In Honour of Newfoundland's Missing During the Great War*. St. John's: Breakwater Books, 2009.

Hesketh-Prichard, Maj. H. *Sniping in France: With Notes on the Scientific Training of Scouts, Observers and Snipers*. London: Hutchinson & Co., 1921.

Lind, Francis T., with Introduction by J. A. Robinson and Foreword by Peter Neary. *The Letters of Mayo Lind*. St. John's: Creative Publishers (Killick Press), 2001.

Macfarlane, David. *The Danger Tree: Memory, War, and The Search For A Family's Past*. Toronto: Macfarlane, Walter & Ross. 1991. Toronto: Random House, 2000. New York: Walker & Company, 2001.

McAllister, Anthony. *The Greatest Gallantry: The Newfoundland Regiment at Monchy-le-Preux April 14, 1917*. St. John's: DRC Publishers, 2010.

Murphy, Tony, and Paul Kenney. *The Trail of the Caribou: Newfoundland in the First World War, 1914-18*. St. John's: Harry Cuff Publishing, 1991.

Nicholson, Gerald W. L. *The Fighting Newfoundlander: A History of the Royal Newfoundland Regiment*. Ottawa: Carleton Library Series, 209, 1964. Montreal: McGill-Queen's University Press, 2006.

Parsons, W. David. *Pilgrimage: A guide to the Royal Newfoundland Regiment in World War One*. St. John's: Creative Publishers, 1994.

Patey, Francis. *Veterans of the North*. St. John's: Creative Publishers, 2003.

Riggs, Bert, ed. *Grand Bank Soldier: The War Letters of Lance Corporal Curtis Forsey*. St. John's: Flanker Press, 2007.

Stacey, Anthony James, and Jean Edwards Stacey. *Memoirs of a Blue Puttee: The Newfoundland Regiment in World War One*. St. John's: DRC Publishers, 2002.

Sullivan, Joan. *In The Field*. St. John's: Breakwater Books, 2012.

Tait, R. H. *The Trail of the Caribou: The Royal Newfoundland Regiment, 1914-1918*. Boston: Newfoundland Publishing Co., 1933.

Author Biographies

Howard Leopold Morry was born into a merchant-class family from Devon that immigrated to the Southern Shore of Newfoundland in the 1700s. Their fortune was wiped out in the bank crash of 1894. He worked for his father without taking a wage until he had paid back every cent to those to whom he owed money. He and his brothers served in different forces in wwi. Howard joined the Royal Newfoundland Regiment, and his experiences serving in Gallipoli, France, and Belgium marked him for life. This is his story.

Christopher J. A. Morry, who was born in Newfoundland, is the grandson of Howard Morry. He worked for almost forty years as a marine and freshwater biologist for the Canadian government, iucn—The World Conservation Union, and in the private sector. For twenty years he has studied his family history, and this is his first book on the subject.